A Circle of Friends

Remembering Madeleine L'Engle

A Circle of Friends

Remembering Madeleine L'Engle

Edited by Katherine Kirkpatrick

A **Circle of Friends** Publication • 2009

Book design by Claudia Graphics, www.claudiagraphics.com.
Text is set in Adobe Garamond Pro and display type in Brioso Pro.

2009 SECOND EDITION (black and white)

Publisher's Cataloging in Publication Data

A Circle of Friends : Remembering Madeleine L'Engle /
edited by Katherine Kirkpatrick.
p. cm.
Summary: Madeleine L'Engle's friends and writing students remember the beloved author in nearly three dozen essays and poems, illustrated with photographs.

1. L'Engle, Madeleine, 1918-2007— Friends and associates - Anecdotes. 2. Authorship – Religious aspects. 3. Christianity and the arts. 4. Creative writing—essays. I. Kirkpatrick, Katherine.

PS 3523 E55 Z47 2009
814 C

ISBN 978-0-557-22788-4

Dedicated to Madeleine L'Engle,
our mentor and friend

Madeleine in a celebratory salute after her granddaughter Charlotte's wedding, August 1996.

Contents

Acknowledgements

"The Journey to Becoming" by Barbara Braver includes previously published material by the same author in *The Swiftly Tilting Worlds of Madeleine L'Engle*, Shaw Publishers, copyright © 1998. "Supper with Madeleine" by Stephanie Cowell is based on an article originally published in *The Living Church Magazine* on May 9, 1999. "Madeleine L'Engle: Writer and Friend—1918–2007" by Luci Shaw includes material previously published by the author as a foreword to Madeleine L'Engle's collected poems, *The Ordering of Love* (WaterBrook/Shaw Books, 2005), and in a memorial article in *Books & Culture,* January 2008. It also contains parts of the memorial address at Madeleine's funeral in Goshen, Connecticut, in September 2007. "Madeleine, Victoria, and Me" by Claire Whitcomb was published in a slightly different form in *Victoria* Magazine in January 1995.

The editor kindly acknowledges permission to reproduce the photos and illustrations on the following pages: pages 8 (bottom), 12, courtesy of Diane Amison-Loring; page 168, courtesy of Terryl Wiley Anderson; pages V, 6, 58 (photo by Steve Vinik), 120, 153, courtesy of Dana Catharine; pages 72, 157 (top), 183, 186, courtesy of Linda Champanier; page 52, courtesy of Carole Chase; pages 5, 11, 48, 112, 156, 157 (bottom), 172, courtesy of the Community of the Holy Spirit; front cover (publicity photo, around 1987) and pages 4, 67, 109 (publicity photo by Toshi Otsuki, 1994), 180, included with the permission of Crosswicks, Ltd., in cooperation with McIntosh & Otis, Inc.; page 47 (top), courtesy of Sandy Hudson; pages 80, 88, 90, 94, 103, 105, 115, 117, 147, 164 (top right), courtesy of Katherine Kirkpatrick; pages 97, 99, 130, courtesy of Pamela Leggett; back cover and pages 15, 17, 18, 21, 70 (top), 84, courtesy of Cornelia Duryée Moore; title page and pages XII, XVI, 24, 28, 31, 34, 42, 47 (bottom), 68, 70 (bottom), 101, 144, 170, 176, 189, 191, courtesy of Luci Shaw; pages 164 (top left), courtesy of Sanna Stanley; pages 8 (top), 61, 62, 83, courtesy of Phyllis White; pages 73, 142, courtesy of Sally Lowe Whitehead; pages 124, 192, courtesy of Beth Vendryes Williams.

All photos of the contributors are courtesy of the individual authors, except for the photograph of Peggy Harrington by Sydney Stafford, included here courtesy of Katherine Kirkpatrick. The photo of Claudia Carlson was taken by Lynn Saville.

Madeleine L'Engle's poem "Within This Strange and Quickened Dust," on page 96, was first published in *Lines Scribbled On an Envelope*, Farrar, Straus and Giroux, copyright ©1969 by Crosswicks, Ltd., and is reprinted with permission of McIntosh & Otis, Inc.

The quotation excerpted on page 126, is reprinted from *The Rock That Is Higher* copyright © 1993, 2003 by Crosswicks. WaterBrook Press, Colorado Springs, CO. All rights reserved.

"The Tallis Canon" (Compline Hymn #43, versus 1–4) is reprinted from *The Hymnal 1982 according to the use of The Episcopal Church*, copyright © 1982, the Church Pension Fund, New York, NY. The words of the first four stanzas are by Thomas Ken (1637–1711) and the last two stanzas by Madeleine L'Engle, included with the permission of Crosswicks, Ltd., in cooperation with McIntosh & Otis, Inc. The music, "The Eighth Tune," is by Thomas Tallis (c. 1505–1585). The lettering is courtesy of Beth Vendryes Williams.

Friends and students of Madeleine L'Engle who would like to contribute to a future print or web-based publication are invited to contact the editor at katherine@katherinekirkpatrick.com.

A Circle of Friends is available in two print-on-demand editions; a gift edition (published in full color) and a general reader's edition (published in black and white). Copies of both editions can be ordered through Lulu.com and Amazon.com.

Madeleine, 1994.

Introduction

by Catherine Grace, CHS

Catherine Grace, CHS, is one of the three leaders of the Community of the Holy Spirit. Sister Catherine Grace helped to create the Community's eco-spiritual education center and working farm at St. Cuthbert's House in the Melrose Convent, Brewster, New York.

Madeleine L'Engle Franklin was a dear friend and devoted Associate of the Community of the Holy Spirit (CHS), an Episcopal religious order for women in New York. Her long relationship with us began shortly after the Community was founded in 1952, before she began teaching at our school. Though convention might say it continued until her death, the truth is that it continues still. Madeleine was unforgettable. She will live forever in the memories and stories of the sisters. Though I was not a part of the early life of this Community, the stories of both Madeleine and our founder Mother Ruth are rife.

Neither woman would ever be described as particularly soft-spoken, shy, or reserved. They were feminists well before the word was commonly used, and each of them left a strong impression wherever she went. One became a world-famous author; the other established a religious order and two still-thriving schools in New York, using her desire and wit to overcome a complete lack of funding.

They are the kind of women who are remembered with warm regard, a broad smile, and the occasional eye-roll.

Madeleine and her husband Hugh were actors, though Madeleine's primary vocation as a writer took over soon after their marriage. Their children—Josephine, Bion, and Maria—all attended school at St. Hilda's & St. Hugh's, which was founded and run by the sisters in New York City.

Soon after her children entered the school, Madeleine began attending retreats offered at the convent and making private retreats there regularly. She and Canon Edward West of the Cathedral of St. John the Divine (another soul I'd affectionately label a certified "character") became fast friends; he held the position of Warden at the convent, and the Cathedral played an important part in the lives of the sisters. West eventually provided the essence of a fictional priest, Canon John Tallis, who appeared in one of Madeleine's book series. The convent and cathedral managed their way into Madeleine's writing as well.

Both the Franklins loved the school and the Community; they helped with the annual school Christmas pageant for years until Madeleine's own career began to take more and more of her time. She was much in demand as a retreat leader and speaker, and even taught a rigorous (and popular) writing class at the school for several years. Madeleine was incredibly generous, both with her time and with her talent. For years she conducted lengthy writers' workshops at both of the Community's houses, in New York City and Brewster, New York. This is how I first met her soon after I arrived at CHS in 1990 and took on the oversight of the retreat and workshop program.

She never asked for or accepted an honorarium for her long, dedicated hours as a workshop or retreat leader for us, and she assigned the profits of at least one book to the Community. In 1975 the sisters' chapel organ was dedicated to her recently deceased mother, and following Hugh's death in 1986, Madeleine established a maintenance fund for the organ in Hugh's memory.

Madeleine was unbelievably persistent. She never allowed her students a second of self-pity upon receiving the dreaded manuscript turn-down. Her own early efforts garnered what may have been a record number of rejections; but she kept right on sending out her work, knowing in her heart that she had something delightful and important to say. Madeleine's never-give-up attitude shines through much of her work and is reflected in the efforts of her many students.

Her writing workshops were wildly popular, and students who had already attended at least one of them always wanted to come back for another. She was strict about limiting the number of participants, and I remember more than one phone call between us where she adamantly stomped her foot with the pronouncement of "Twenty, and *no more,* my dear!"

Many were the weepy pleas I received from prospective students who were not allowed into the workshop. I finally designed a method to quietly "arrange" it so at least half of each class consisted of new people. If Madeleine figured out my subterfuge, she never mentioned it.

Not only was Madeleine a creative and talented writer, she was a superb teacher. What I remember best about her is that she limited her classes for an excellent reason: every single piece of writing created by every single participant was carefully read, reflected upon, and commented on by Madeleine. I was never able to attend any of her classes, but I had frequent conversations with students who did, and without exception these people loved her, were devoted to her, and learned a great deal at her feet.

Annual alumni gatherings and ongoing writing support groups of "Madeleine grads" flourished. Besides helping each other continually improve their skills, the grads always celebrated Madeleine's November birthday. Many still do, as I understand.

This lovely book's essays will fill in many of the blanks in this brief foreword. You may recognize the names of some of the contributors from your own reading experience, for many of her students have become published authors themselves. This collection is one small way her loving and loyal followers can share their skills and their affection for this great woman with the rest of us.

May you read with pleasure.

Madeleine in the Cathedral Library, 1989.

Editor's Note

Madeleine L'Engle (1918-2007) published sixty books in her lifetime, including children's and adult fiction, poetry, essays, and biographical books. Several more titles have been released posthumously.

She began teaching writing in 1960 when her children attended St. Hilda's & St. Hugh's School. She continued to host workshops at the convent affiliated with this school for the next forty years (while also teaching in other church-affiliated locations all over the U.S., Canada, and occasionally abroad). Madeleine became more active as a teacher in the late 1980s, when she was widowed; I was one of her students during this time period, starting in her Community of the Holy Spirit workshop in 1989. She continued teaching until the mid to late 1990s, when her health declined.

For many of her students, the first surprise came in the form of the workshop setting—an Episcopal convent in Manhattan—where the writers attended evening prayers and shared a meal with the sisters. As an associate lay member of CHS, Madeleine held her workshop in the convent partly to raise funds for the nuns. She also enjoyed the atmosphere of the convent. Nearly forty years after Madeleine's children graduated from St. Hilda's & St. Hugh's, the convent remained an integral part of her life.

Another surprise lay in Madeleine's unconventional manner of instruction. "Write for an hour, don't think," she said. "Attempts to direct only interfere in creative work." Rarely did she provide specific pointers about technique, and she never commented on how one might go about submitting a manuscript to an agent or editor.

Many students were drawn to Madeleine's classes because of the vivid and original storytelling in her fantasy novels. Tall and stately, the author physically projected that same sense of wonder. She wore long dresses made of colorful fabrics. Her expansive vision included a belief in angels, whom she was sure appeared regularly in everyone's lives. She regarded the imaginative themes and creatures in her books as expressions of the truth. (She said a story could still be *"true* without being *factual."*) She spoke of God's love as the ultimate truth at the heart of creation, the same force that holds the galaxies in place.

Madeleine often talked about stories unfolding in their own time. She'd use the same phrases to describe God's plan in individual lives. "We don't always know where the story is going. We don't need to."

She referred to our human view of time, "the short view," as *Chronos.* Time from God's perspective, "the long view," was *Kairos* (both are Greek words). "Sometimes we can glimpse *Kairos,*" she said. "Truth is eternal; we can slip into the eternal. And story is truth." Writing stories was one of the ways, according to Madeleine, that we can collaborate with divine purpose.

Such lofty talk set the atmosphere in Madeleine's classes. Madeleine's wise and loving presence brought out the best in people. The convent gatherings became fertile ground for stories and poems. Many participants went on to publish books. But the experience wasn't about publishing; that was merely a fortuitous by-product of diligently pursuing one's craft. Though writing was the context, the participants formed connections on a spiritual level, and it was this shared journey that ultimately mattered. Friendships grew and blossomed. Three of the contributors in this book met their spouses through Madeleine. (Did the nuns ever imagine their chapel would be used for weddings?)

Generally after each workshop concluded, a new writers' group was born. These groups met in various homes, and periodically, the small groups came together to share writing in a larger group meeting. Over time, this larger group became a community of more than a hundred writers. The writers attended each other's book signings and other events, and Madeleine participated in these occasions whenever she could take time away from her busy schedule of lecturing all over the world. And once a year, Madeleine invited all her workshop alumni to a party in her large, elegant Manhattan apartment for fellowship and feasting.

After Madeleine's death in 2007, I yearned for her and those gatherings. I also felt a profound need to go to at least one of her memorial services. But I'd long since left the East Coast for Seattle, and the responsibility of caring for two young children kept me from attending either of the services. I found myself on the phone a lot with my writers' group friends in New York. The idea popped into my head one day, "Why don't we write a book about Madeleine?"

First I contacted my closest friends. Then I took out the contact list of Madeleine's CHS "alumni" that I'd received at one of her gatherings, and picked up the phone. The list was fifteen years old, and as is natural for a group of people living in Manhattan, the majority of writers had moved on, to different apartments or out of the city.

Occasionally someone answered the phone and I reintroduced myself. These writers all seemed to remember me because I'd been a "regular" at Madeleine's workshops and retreats. Nearly everyone I talked to immediately took to the idea of being part of a book. Soon word spread, and other writers began contacting me.

Some former workshop participants, by this time, had become successful authors, but I did not "pick and choose" my contributors. If someone on the list answered the phone, or came to me through another venue related to Madeleine, then they were "qualified." (I was certain Madeleine would have extended the same invitation. Besides, Madeleine often talked of the great heroes of the Bible as being "*un*qualified"—another of her favorite themes.)

So by my free-flowing, not very organized method of doing business, I no doubt failed to invite many writers who took the workshops and would have loved to participate in the book. To do the project over, I'd make more of an effort to locate Madeleine's former students at St. Hilda's & St. Hugh's school, her numerous godchildren, and those who took her workshops in various locations across the country; perhaps one day we can publish a subsequent volume.

Some contributors came to me a year before the book was to be published; others only a month before. In some cases I did "hand holding" and helped or cajoled writers through multiple drafts; in other cases the prose came in so perfectly I didn't change a word. To my great delight, a few of Madeleine's closest friends and fellow writers joined the enterprise, adding dimension to its scope.

The project turned into a much larger, and different sort of endeavor than I'd imagined. I began to make friends through e-mail whom I've never met in person. And to my great joy, it happened on numerous occasions that I was able to put old friends in contact with one another. Some of them have now met in person for the first time in years. For many of the contributors, who were quite close to Madeleine and are still mourning her death, the creation of this book has offered an opportunity for reflection, re-connection with old friends, healing, and renewal.

That our book would have pleased Madeleine greatly, I have no doubt. I think even more than the literary aspect of the project, she would have celebrated the communal aspect of her students coming together in friendship. I'd often heard Madeleine say that the meeting of friends (especially over a candle-lit meal) was a "foretaste of heaven."

Madeleine was proud of her students' dedication to each other. She once said, after surviving a near-fatal car crash in California, "God must have kept me alive in order to foster community." In this public talk, given to the American Library Association, Madeleine mentioned some of "her writers" by name, along with their accomplishments.

Madeleine also formed lasting bonds with writers and students in many other places aside from New York City. She taught regularly at the Community of the Holy Spirit's second convent house in Brewster, New York; Holy

Cross Monastery on the Hudson River in New York; Mt. Calvary Monastery in Santa Barbara, California; Vancouver School of Theology and Regent College in Vancouver, British Columbia; Wheaton College (where her manuscripts and correspondence are archived) in Wheaton, Illinois; and Mundelein College in Chicago, Illinois.

A Circle of Friends includes reminiscences by Madeleine' students and mentees, as well as her closest writing friends and contemporaries, many in overlapping roles. To all, Madeleine became a transformational light.

The proceeds of this book will be donated to the Community of the Holy Spirit.

—Katherine Kirkpatrick, August 2009

A Circle of Friends
Remembering Madeleine L'Engle

For Madeleine

by Dana Catharine

Dana Catharine first met Madeleine L'Engle and her husband, Hugh Franklin, as a student at St. Hilda's & St. Hugh's in 1960 at the age of fourteen. She is the author of To Fly with the Swallows, *a book about old California, and co-author with Richard Larios of* La Causa, *a children's biography of Cesar Chavez.*

I called Madeleine L'Engle my godmother, but what exactly is a godmother? In religion, a godmother, a godparent, is someone who promises to look after the spiritual health of the baby, to lead and direct that growing person in the paths of righteousness.

In story, a godmother, a fairy godmother, looks after other kinds of well being, providing, for instance, a carriage and white horses for the ball.

Madeleine L'Engle was both kinds to me, and neither.

She was not present at my baptism. And she most certainly was not a fairy tale character! But she was, perhaps, the most important influence on both my spiritual and physical lives.

Madeleine and her husband, the actor Hugh Franklin, walked into the world of our small, conservative, Upper West Side school, St. Hilda's & St. Hugh's, run by the Community of the Holy Spirit, when I was fourteen. The high church Episcopal nuns were, in those long-ago days, old-fashioned, repressive, very British, fierce, loving, generous, dedicated, strict, demanding—we sang full Anglican Morning Prayer every day, forty-five minutes of Anglican Chant. We ourselves were habited in navy blue and grey.

Madeleine and Hugh were like a pair of elegant and intelligent giraffes (like the startling, innovative creatures the director Julie Taymor designed for the Broadway production of *The Lion King*): tall, astonishing, full of élan vital—and more important, a contagious sense of *joie de vivre.*

It was their job to teach us drama; they took on the direction of the Christmas Pageant, a solemn and beloved event revered by everyone in the school—not something cute involving small children in bathrobes, but a production scripted by St. Luke, scored by the Medieval masters, and set in the Cathedral of St. John

Hugh and Madeleine, around 1977.

the Divine. They took something beautiful, and added their spirit and grace, their love and excitement, and made it something glorious. Madeleine often spoke of the glory of directing the Three Kings down the aisle of the Cathedral, which was the length of two New York City blocks. Under their direction, I played the alto recorder in the Choir stalls—all the verses of "O Come, O Come, Emmanuel"—and later played St. Elizabeth welcoming the Virgin Mary and her news of the birth of the Savior.

And it was their job to teach us Speech. They challenged us, they dared us, they stretched us, they terrified us. Speak about a dramatic moment in your life, speak about something you care about passionately, defend your life.

Once they gave us an assignment based on the idea that extraterrestrials had taken over the planet, and to save our lives, each of us must say why we deserved to live. Saturated in the mistaken idea of "love your neighbor *instead* of yourself," and the gory and glorious stories of the early Christian martyrs, we gave lame and pathetic speeches about our unworthiness, and that we were ready to be disposed of, so that the next fellow might live. We were total failures.

Madeleine and Hugh were mystified, saddened, and upset. They re-directed. They explained that we must show why we deserved to live in our own right, not *instead* of someone else. They gave us another chance. Then, we began to get it. I was able to articulate my own belief about life, which had grown from my experience of severe illness. I remembered the first day I was allowed, after six months of high fever, to go to Riverside Park. Every stick and stone and dirty city sparrow seemed to me the most spectacular thing I had ever seen. I had escaped from a dark prison, and my purpose was to rejoice in the beauty of this earth. I spoke as a poet, incorporating Emily's speech from *Our Town*, "Oh, earth, you're too wonderful for anyone to realize you."

Madeleine and Hugh asked us to recognize our worth and to value our own lives. They helped us begin to realize who we were, and encouraged us to be.

Madeleine and Hugh were our teachers. But they did not teach us with their words alone; they taught us with their lives. Teaching isn't really about teaching a subject—we can learn most things on our own, if we want to. Teaching is really about showing students that it is all right to grow up, to be alive and interested. Some wise person said, "You don't teach a subject, you teach who you are." The *who* of Madeleine and Hugh shouted out who they were. They were multicultural before the term was coined, rejoicing in the colors and textures and flavors of the world. They were lovers of words and story and language, of creation and community, sitting down to a dinner table where everyone was welcomed.

They were bright shining stars—oh yes, he was on Broadway, and she won awards for her books, but for us, they were the stars that lit our way. Being with them, and around them, and in their light, allowed me to be and breathe, and helped me begin to become who I am.

Madeleine was an active and involved part of my life from then on. Somehow I was absorbed into their family of three children, and numerous dogs and cats.

Then began the dinners together, singing grace, hands around the table, full of conversation, laughter, music, and story. I was a shy, quiet kind of kid. But in the Franklin household, full of actors and artists, you could not get a word in edgewise at the family dinner table if you did not project. Madeleine and Hugh taught me to speak, to speak up, to speak out, to speak boldly—to speak up for myself and for what I believe in, to make myself heard.

When I ask my students to sit up and speak out, it is because that is what they taught me. If you are going to say something, then SAY IT so that it can be heard!

There were also summer visits to Crosswicks, their home in northwestern Connecticut. When I spent time with them, I slept in the attic bedroom that Meg Murry's was based on, usually with a kitten at my feet.

Madeleine taught me many things over summer evenings playing charades, ping-pong, and Murder in the Dark, telling jokes and ghost stories, and making pie beds (notably, for the Dean of the Cathedral of the Incarnation in Long Island, an old mutual friend), visits to the hidden brook where we read evening prayer—the psalm for one day read, "Save me, O God, for the waters are come in, even unto my soul," and then it absolutely poured rain over us. Peals of laughter. Evenings spent singing favorite hymns, and bawdy, silly French songs, "Madame la Marquise," "Chevaliers de la Table Ronde," lying in

Madeleine and Canon Edward West.

the tall grass, just staring at the sky and the overhanging tree branches. And yes, we would get up in the middle of the night and make hot chocolate and talk about the great questions; or lie out on the old New England rocks and look up at the stars, singing all the songs we knew with stars in them. She gave me my first prayer book, and she gave me Crosswicks for my honeymoon.

It all sounds idyllic, but it was human, too, with all the human flaws we create. There was, of course, a dark side, which all the songs, and games, and laughter, and hot chocolate tried to keep at bay.

People often ask me if I am a character in her books. The answer is no.

But I was probably influenced by those characters. I am probably more like some of them now than I was then. But she did write me into her nonfiction books, and she often wrote poems for my birthday. Some of those have been published.

Although I was her daughter's age, I stepped forward and she stepped back and we met somewhere outside of *Chronos*, in a place of exuberant love and joy.

She was mentor and guide—words too small to describe the impact that she had on my life—and she was most lovingly what she liked to call me, godfriend.

I felt that we could speak of anything to each other, and that was an enormous relief.

Madeleine often spoke of life and the afterlife as being like school—school in the very best sense of the word—where you learned and moved on from grade to grade, Heaven being a kind of post-doctoral study. There is a line from the Episcopal prayers for the Dead that supports her idea: *"May they go from strength to strength."*

Madeleine, may you go from strength to strength, surrounded by stars...

Thank you for the blessing of your light.

Dana Catharine, Madeleine, Madeleine's daughter Josephine, and Cornelia Duryée Moore, around 1996.

Memories of Madeleine: A Glimpse into *Kairos*

by Diane Amison-Loring

Diane Amison-Loring was a member of the Community of the Holy Spirit for thirty-one years. A longtime children's book librarian, she lives and works in Connecticut.

On July 3, 1965, when I was almost nineteen years old, I moved from Minnesota to New York City and entered the Community of the Holy Spirit (CHS) as a postulant. Just a year before, Madeleine L'Engle had accepted her Newbery Medal for *A Wrinkle in Time*. Madeleine had become an Associate of CHS, and in this same time period, she taught creative writing to the seniors at St. Hilda's & St. Hugh's School. All three of Madeleine and Hugh's children were out of high school at the time. Josephine had graduated from St. Hilda's in 1963. Madeleine was in her late forties.

When I joined CHS, I had never heard of Madeleine L'Engle and had not read any of her books. Where I'd come from in the Midwest, word of her work had not spread. I remember the beauty of the first St. Hilda's & St. Hugh's School Christmas pageant I saw at the Cathedral of St. John the Divine. Madeleine was its director. The music was medieval, the costumes colorful, and the actors in this mime brought the Christmas story to life on a very grand scale. Madeleine was dressed flamboyantly in colorful clothing and long skirts. She wore a large fur coat and fur hat because of the intense cold in the Cathedral.

Who was this elegant woman? One of my fellow postulants was a graduate of St. Hilda's and knew Madeleine very well. She often spoke of the creative writing classes she had taken with Madeleine. This postulant had also read Madeleine's books and some of her as yet unpublished poetry. I remember the copy of *A Wrinkle in Time* that finally made its way up to the novitiate library. I had to wait a long time before I had a turn to read it. Sometimes at recreation times, I learned more about Madeleine's house, Crosswicks, and the fun that happened there during the summers. I listened to stories about the young women who gathered at Madeleine's apartment on West End Avenue to listen to music and to critique

Cathedral Close, the Cathedral of Saint John the Divine, a second home to Madeleine for more than forty years.

Diane Amison-Loring as sister Mary Veronica, CHS.

each other's writing. I wanted to learn more about Madeleine. I wanted to get to know Madeleine.

In the fall of 1966, St. Hilda's & St. Hugh's School opened its new building on West 114th Street in Manhattan. Mother Ruth, the reverend mother and founder of the order, decided that the rather large novitiate, a group of about twelve women, needed to have different courses of study in theology, Bible study, liturgy, and the arts. One of the courses would be creative writing.

The room we used was the music theory room on the second floor. It was a very warm room, and after a long day working with children, it was hard for the postulants and novices to stay awake. Madeleine set the room on fire. We wrote for her and shyly read our work to each other. Madeleine helped us explore this new life that we were testing. She encouraged us to keep journals. Madeleine's love for words could be summed up by a verse she liked to quote (by "one of her favorite authors, Anon"):

> The written word
> Should be clean as bone,
> Clear as light,
> Firm as stone.
> Two words are not as good as one.

Madeleine shared her love of God with the novitiate and let us see a little bit of her life as a writer. We were fascinated.

When I finished my novitiate, I was sent to Columbia University's School of General Studies in order to complete my B.A. I majored in English literature with an emphasis on the nineteenth century. I had really wanted to become a librarian, but when I had entered the Community of the Holy Spirit in 1965, the Community already had two sisters who were librarians working in the schools run by the order and didn't need another. In 1971, after I completed my undergraduate education, instead of going on to library school, I was assigned to teach the seventh grade at St. Hilda's.

In 1967, Madeleine had given me a copy of her newly

published drama *The Journey with Jonah* as a present for my first profession. How could I best honor that gift but to stage the play with the seventh graders I taught? Madeleine had directed the first performance at St. Hilda's while her daughter Josephine was a student. My seventh graders rose to the challenge and learned their roles. We presented the play for the end of school. Madeleine came to the performance.

Years followed in rhythm with Madeleine coming and going to and from the convent for Vespers, to give retreats to associates, for Advent conversations, for Christmas Eve, and for Lenten talks. One year, Mother Mary Christabel, the Superior who served after Mother Ruth, decided that every sister should have a spiritual director and directed all of the life professed sisters to choose a person outside of the Community for that purpose. I asked Madeleine if she would be my spiritual director, and after discussion, she agreed. This decision was one of the most important ones I ever made.

Spiritual direction with Madeleine L'Engle was like going to draw water from a deep well. With her help, I drew water that was so cold and crisp I could never get enough of it. She reflected truths that helped me grow as a Religious. Her loyalty to and love for the Community of the Holy Spirit was a safety net that took me through some difficult transition times. We walked through years of light and darkness. These were years that included three major transition times for me. In 1979, I was transferred to the Melrose School, CHS's school in Brewster, New York, to teach; in 1985, I was asked to quit classroom teaching and enter library school; and in September 1986, I was transferred back to New York City. Whenever I called her, either at her home or at her office, the Cathedral Library at St. John the Divine, Madeleine would pick up the phone and her "Madeleine" or "Library" greeting was reassuring. Madeleine never put down the day-to-day stuff of life that came into our conversations. She used it to show how God was working.

Madeleine pushed me beyond what I thought I could do. She expressed doubt over some of my choices, but upheld me as I tried to live out the vow of obedience. She was there to help pick up the pieces when I just couldn't do something, most notably when I undertook the task of teaching the second grade at Melrose. She was a source of stability that helped me stand fast as the church and my Community moved away from the conservative ideals I hold. I cherished Madeleine's help as the Community tried out ways of worship different from what I had known and loved, and discarded the traditional language I used in my own daily private prayers.

Madeleine was one of those rare individuals who could understand both sides of an issue, even if she held a strong opinion on one side. I had some difficulty at first with the concept of women's ordination. Madeleine explained the call to the priesthood as a call to the individual soul, without regard to gender. Madeleine usually counseled waiting on decisions, because things would change around me. Her loving mantra was that God would give me strength to bear whatever difficulties came my way. Madeleine liked to quote from *Meet the Austins* when things seemed tough: "Bless you, God, for being God!"

In 1985, when I had the opportunity to go back to college and earn a Master's in Library Science, Long Island University offered the option of a Master's thesis as part of the degree process. I chose to survey Madeleine's entire literary output to 1987. I studied the way that Madeleine opened the field of children's literature to subjects that society considered inappropriate for the young. Madeleine dared to broach issues that affect young people such as the death of a parent, divorce, and adoption. She liked to define a children's book this way: "It is a book a child will read." Madeleine worked with me and gave me precious time, even though I was writing my thesis during the months when her husband, Hugh, was dying of cancer.

When I was the librarian at Xavier High School, a Jesuit high school in Manhattan, I sometimes stopped at Madeleine's apartment for spiritual direction before I went home for Vespers. When the Advent conversations were held at CHS, Madeleine liked to have me stop by on my way home from work and walk her to the convent.

One wintry afternoon, I reached Madeleine's West End apartment building and picked her up, and we turned the corner onto West End Avenue. A man came running up to us and pulled on a small purse that Madeleine had hung around her neck. The cord snapped and the man ran away with the purse. Madeleine was shaken and furious. She shouted after him, "God will get you!"

I ran after the man, shouting, "Stop, thief! The man is a thief, stop him!"

Bystanders looked on, and the man kept running.

I had to stop. I couldn't run fast enough to catch him.

Madeleine turned back to her apartment building to ask the doorman to call the police. Then she called the convent to say we would be late. The police came, questioned us, and got a description of the man.

Who could guess what happened next? The thief kept running, but he didn't know the area at all. He grabbed something else from someone, took the contents of Madeleine's purse, and threw the purse away. He saw that people were pursuing him, saw the wall that divides the houses from Riverside Park, and jumped over it. What he didn't know was that the drop on the other side of the wall at that point was twenty feet. He broke a leg and lay there on the ground, where the police came and picked him up.

Madeleine in publity photo, 1970s.

Madeleine took a taxi to the convent for Vespers, supper, and the Advent Conversations. I got in a police car and was driven into Riverside Park. I identified the thief. Yes, God had "got him."

After I left the convent in July 1996, Madeleine and I talked, but less often than before. Life in the world takes a lot of time when it comes to earning a living. I worked two jobs in order to be able to pay my debts. In time, I moved out of Manhattan to Long Island, then to upstate New York, and finally to Danbury, Connecticut. Madeleine's friendship followed me like the proverbial "red thread" connecting those who are destined to meet.

When Madeleine went to live in the nursing home in Litchfield, Connecticut, I visited her. She was so tired that she could not open her eyes except once to see me. I prayed with her and sat beside her bed for a while. It reminded me of the many times she had listened to me in that way back in her Manhattan apartment.

I brought my husband to see her. Bill Loring is a priest who knew Madeleine well. Bill blessed her and prayed for her. That was the last time we saw Madeleine on this earth. She is waiting for us. I pray that she will be one of the people in the greeting committee when we come to the gates of Heaven.

Father Bill Loring and Diane Amison-Loring.

Madeleine L'Engle, *Anam Chara*

by Cornelia Duryée Moore

Cornelia Duryée Moore feels privileged to have been Madeleine's friend and godchild for nearly thirty years. She is a wife, mother, writer, director, and filmmaker. Her award-winning feature film The Dark Horse *is currently in film festivals. Her Seattle-based production company, Kairos Productions, is currently in early pre-production on her second feature film,* Camilla Dickinson, *based on Madeleine's book* Camilla.

I woke up from yet another mourning dream about Madeleine in the deep dark of a recent dawn. In it, there was impossibly sad, yet impossibly glorious music, with the words "Holy, Holy, Holy, Lord God Almighty" sung over and over by the very air, and running through every cell of me. Now, to my utter sorrow, I cannot remember the tune (which was nothing like the usual one we hear). I pray I will remember it some day. I lay there sobbing for at least an hour, alone in the bed (as my husband was visiting relatives that weekend), and aching to talk to Madeleine one more time.

I think in pictures much of the time; it may be why I am a filmmaker. In this dream I saw, over and over, certain scenes from my life with Madeleine. The first one was the day I met her, when I was in college and attended Madeleine's book signing at the Secret Garden Bookstore in Seattle. In her lap I placed a first edition of *The Small Rain* that I had had traced by Shorey's Bookstore at great expense. At that time it had been out of print for a very long time. She gaped at it in wonder, and then asked, "Where did you get this? I haven't seen one of these for decades." I smiled and said, "I had to have them all, I had it traced." (This was, of course, in the days before the Internet, when it was more difficult to trace books.)

Later that weekend, Madeleine was truly exhausted after the third seminar she had given, and she said she felt like a "Squishy Pumpkin." The next night she and I talked, over my "Anti-Squishy-Pumpkin Kit," a basket full of comestibles that I had created and given her to try to help ease her exhaustion, and she

---

Anam Chara means "soul friend" in Irish Gaelic.

invited me to come study writing with her at Mundelein College in Chicago that summer for two weeks.

I was accepted by the college, and I spent a sacred two weeks as her student, along with thirty or so folks older than myself, earning my first graduate credit in a course called "Story: Vehicle for Truth"; eating dinner with Madeleine many times as one of the blessed friends she invited often up to her room in the Mundelein convent, dancing a worship dance for the community, and finally believing, through her encouragement, that I could write.

So began the friendship, and so it continued, through many summers at Mundelein, many silent retreats with the Community of the Holy Spirit in New York, and many voyages on my parents' boat. Several decades of two-week boat trips with the Franklins began that first Mundelein summer, during which Madeleine had daily, praise-singing encounters with dolphins as they played in our wake, and during which her husband Hugh ate his first-ever freshly-caught seafood and went into ecstasies, was recognized as a soap star by gushing local ladies in remote B.C. fishing villages, and taught us to play Spite and Malice (a sort of competitive Solitaire game) with great glee. Madeleine and my father were two months apart in age, and had a similar sense of humor, and she and my mother got along like merry and passionately volatile cousins. There were trips nearly every summer thereafter.

There were many school vacations in which I flew to then-terrifying New York City to stay in the little bedroom on the back hall in Madeleine's apartment, and work in the beloved, dusty, creaky, dog-filled Cathedral of Saint John the Divine Library (I did not know those vacations were an audition). There was the winter vacation in which Madeleine told me that I was not really a Presbyterian, I was an Episcopalian, with my love for liturgy and all things canonical, and that I ought to take Confirmation classes. When you are confirmed in the Episcopal Church as an adult, you choose your own godparents. During the following spring break, as we sat and chatted before dinner one warm evening, I was told in no uncertain terms that if I did not choose Madeleine and Hugh, I would never be invited to stay with them again. Madeleine took her role as godmother very seriously, stating often that godparents are responsible to help spiritually form their godchildren. She prayed for her growing list of godchildren daily (I was often a part of these prayers, as we said Compline together most evenings). Madeleine also insisted that I consider becoming an Associate of the Community of the Holy Spirit, as I needed a daily Rule of Life. I did, I do, and I am a proud and grateful Associate to this day.

Early in our friendship, Madeleine taught me the ancient monastic prayer

Madeleine with Sylvia and Phil Duryée aboard the "P.S."

called "the Jesus Prayer." It is simply "Lord Jesus Christ, have mercy on me." She taught me to pray it as a sort of default mode, so that it became as much a part of me as breathing; so that when I woke from a nightmare (as both she and I often did), it became the thread that I held to: saying the name of Jesus over and over. It has indeed become, as Madeleine taught me, a kind of blessing and supplication at once. It becomes an intercession when I think of others while praying it. It is one of her greatest gifts to me, and to many of her friends.

One stormy night in my early twenties, I lay in bed in "Meg's" attic bedroom in Crosswicks and prayed that prayer, looking lovingly at the wide floorboards, the tattered floral wallpaper, and the stored toys and clothes, and feeling the familiar sense of safety and joy that was typical of our times together. I began to have an intuition that I might possibly be relocating to the East Coast. I tucked it away in my mind.

That summer Madeleine, on yet another boat voyage with my parents, looked up from the novel she was writing at the sunny dinette table, over to the nearly unsittable sleeper sofa where I was attempting a poem, and said "Cornelia. I need an assistant. Why don't you come work for me?"

And so I became her "personal assistant," as she called me, and migrated to New York City, where I lived for nearly a decade. For the first year I worked for Madeleine half the day and taught at St. Hilda's & St. Hugh's the other half, studying acting at night. I was privileged to help Sister Heléna Marie direct their glorious Pageant that year; the one that Madeleine and Hugh had devised so long before, set in the Cathedral of St. John the Divine. Madeleine loved hearing about the rehearsals and attended the performance. In subsequent years I worked more hours in the Cathedral and traveled to many of her engagements. I convinced Madeleine, who was at that time feeling a bit lonely worshipping in the large Cathedral congregation on Sundays, that she should follow me down to the more intimate All Angels' Church, and she came, and was soon very involved in that community. We always attended mid-week Eucharist at the Cathedral, and she managed to be a congregant of three congregations at once: the Cathedral, All Angels', and her beloved Congregational Church in Goshen.

I worked hard in the Cathedral Library, because, as many said, Madeleine got more done in one day than most people accomplish in four. She was impossible to keep up with, though I did my best. We worked on her enormous pile of correspondence, which she tried womanfully to answer personally. I set up many of her traveling engagements and traveled with her to try to ease her way a bit, often needing to coax her to rest from the attention of many enthusiastic and loving folk. At every single speaking engagement we attended, someone would ask her, "Where do you get your ideas?" I never understood that question, but it used to amuse her greatly.

Madeleine had the capacity to be close to numerous friends—many of whom I still am privileged to know. She loved us, and we loved her right back. I was often at the Franklins' apartment for meals, as I lived right down the street, and I thoroughly enjoyed the frequent and delightful Franklin parties. After Hugh's death, when Madeleine's brilliant and delightful granddaughters, Léna and Charlotte, moved in for some years, the parties got even more lively. Madeleine, of course, loved being a hostess; loved cooking; loved candlelight dinners and music and hilarity; at least until that time of night when she got that tired "Squishy Pumpkin" look and began to threaten to play her much-dreaded atonal Bartok music on the piano, and it was time to either usher folks out, or tell them to keep the noise way down, and slink off to pray Compline in her bedroom.

Madeleine often expressed to her close friends her great sadness over how her books were received by certain sections of the Christian Church. She often said that she was a kind of "fundamentalist," because the Bible was fundamental to her faith, but then made the distinction that she was not a "Fundalit" (a "Fundamentalist-Literalist"). It was folk from that particular stripe of faith who often accused her of not being a good Christian because, among other things, *A Wrinkle in Time* had a mention of a "Mrs Which" (which was of course a pun/joke, as the Mrs W's revealed strong angelic overtones as the book developed). They objected to Madeleine's sense of humor and to her puns and images. It deeply upset Madeleine, as she and all those close to her knew that she had written it for God. She wrote in *A Circle of Quiet* about her long struggle to get *Wrinkle* published, and about some of the controversy it caused. It was written in 1959, the year I was born. Madeleine and I joked often about that while I worked for her, saying that that year produced a "good vintage."

Madeleine steering the "P.S."

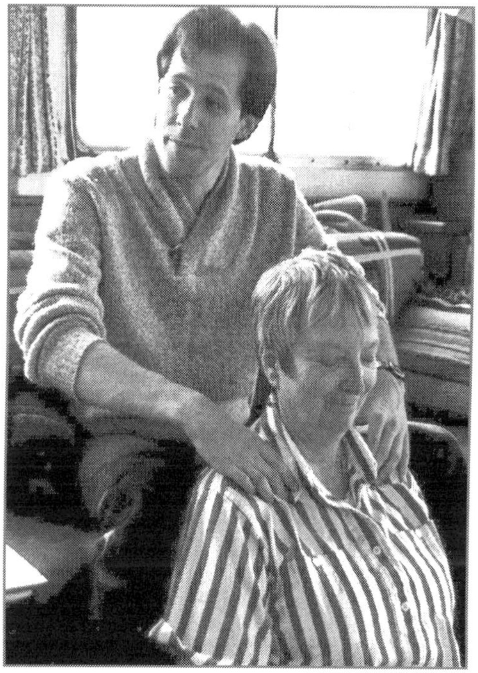

Terry Moore and Madeleine.

Oh how I miss those years in New York when I was friend and godchild and employee, and those intimate, adventurous trips on the boat exploring the North Coast, and the nightly prayers; the encouragement she gave me for over half my life. I miss her every day. Madeleine was always a bit grumpy about me leaving New York, but in a sense it was her own fault; she was always trying to set me up on dates with young men she knew, and I went out with several of her other close friends. And indeed Madeleine was the glue that brought me together with my husband of twenty years, actor Terry Edward Moore.

Terry and I first met at her 70th birthday party. And since he lived in Minnesota and I lived in Manhattan, we knew almost immediately that someone would soon have to move if we were getting serious about this marriage idea. Madeleine was very curious about our courtship, and was playful and triumphant the morning we finally announced that we had proposed to each other, on the last day of a ten-day boat trip. And she threw us a heavenly catered wedding reception for fifty guests in her apartment as a wedding present. Our honeymoon was at a writing retreat she gave at Holy Cross Monastery, in upstate New York, which was full of joy and silliness, as the monks smilingly gave us the only double bed in the entire monastery. And Terry was almost her match; verbally, joyously

The day Cornelia Duryée and Terry Moore became engaged on the "P.S."; left to right, Cornelia, her mother Sylvia, Terry, Madeleine, and Phil, July 1989.

debating over dinners at her apartment, at ping-pong when visiting Crosswicks (though no one could truly ever beat her), or at Spite and Malice or Charades (which is most hilarious with several actors playing) on the boat.

Alas, my two lives did not reconcile permanently. After nine months in Manhattan it became clear that my new husband, who was from a small town in the Midwest, could no longer stand the pace of the city. (Terry is rather like Midwestern-born Hugh was in certain ways, as Madeleine remarked over and over.) We

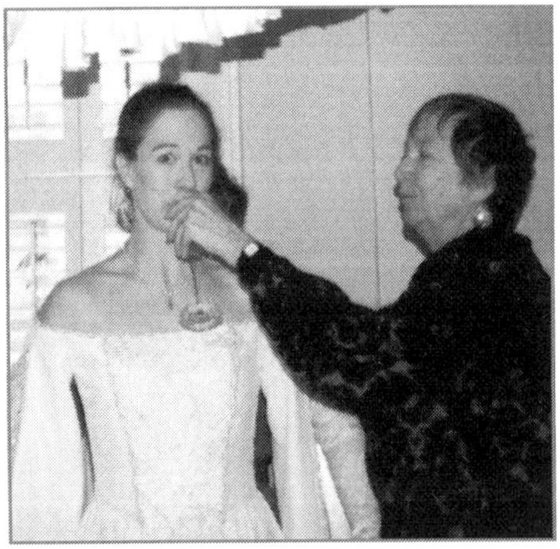

Madeleine offers Cornelia champagne at her wedding reception, January 1990.

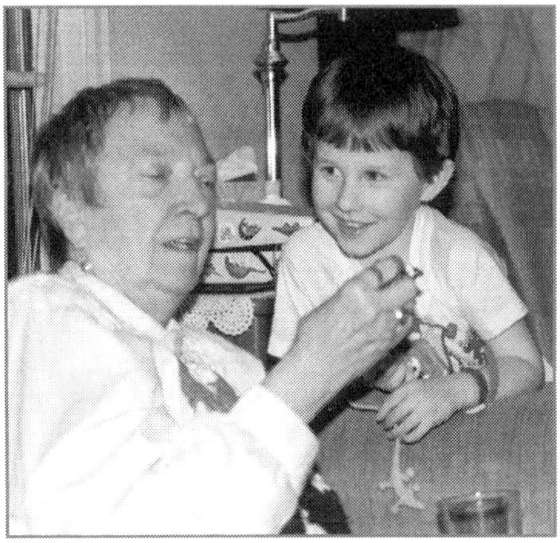

Madeleine and Tallis Moore, around 1995.

moved away to my hometown of Seattle, with the promise that I would be back many times a year to visit. Once again I became a regular guest in the Franklin apartment (but in a different bedroom now); once again I was a regular attendee at Madeleine's silent retreats and writers' workshops, and stayed at Crosswicks, or Crosswicks Cottage, every summer, and the boat voyages continued. Madeleine's dear friend Canon Edward West, who inhabited the office adjacent to hers in the Cathedral all those years, died in 1990, and our son Tallis was named for him soon after that, and for the character he inspired in her books. Madeleine cried in mixed joy and sadness when I called her to tell her Tallis' name. Our second son was named (Mister) Theo, after another of her characters.

In the first year of my marriage, while my husband was working in our new theater in Seattle, Madeleine and I were on the boat one summer, and I watched her write the entire first draft of a novel in two weeks. It was called *Certain Women.* She often wrote prodigiously when on the boat; it seemed to be an inspiring place for her, but this was a new record. As was her wont, she kindly asked me to read the manuscript on the last night of the trip, and I was astonished to read a story featuring a young actress in Manhattan with long red hair, grey eyes, and many eerily-familiar attributes and experiences; mixed, among other things, with her own memories of her acting career on Broadway in the 1940s. It was also set on an extremely-familiar boat... I went up to breakfast the next day rather white-faced, and said to her that of course I thought it was all right to set the novel on P.S. (the boat we were currently aboard), but that it made me very uncomfortable to have the protagonist so very, um, like me... and in many subsequent drafts the parts that were squirmingly familiar faded back to a tolerable level. In watching many of her novels evolve over the years, I learned that many others had come to her and asked for slightly less-incisive character influences.

On one visit to the New York apartment, my young son Tallis told Madeleine that he had been terrified of dogs ever since one bit his hand stealing a cookie, so Madeleine told Tino, her spiritually advanced dog, to "tame" Tallis, in Tallis' hearing. Tino slowly edged closer and closer to Tallis, taming him like the Little Prince and the fox. And by the end of that week, Tallis and Tino were rolling all over the floor of her apartment, giggling and barking. Madeleine often "assigned" beings to each other in this way.

Sometimes when I was visiting New York and "Hotel Madeleine" was full, I would stay at my beloved Community of the Holy Spirit Convent, and walk down to see her for our long, lovely candle-lit dinners, or trips to the ballet or opera, or walks on the Cathedral Close. We always prayed Compline together, whether we were in New York or in Goshen.

Madeleine encouraged me to go to seminary, and gave me my first stole. My first act as a newly ordained minister was serving the two of us the Eucharist on a stormy night in Crosswicks Cottage, wearing the stole. Madeleine was always utterly generous in prayer; she opened her heart to God and to her prayer partners in equal measure. One felt the Spirit singing in the very air; there was pure love; there was Home.

On one lazy afternoon in the 1990s when I was visiting her in the city, we were talking about my recent adaptation and production of a play in Seattle. She got up from her throne of a chair in the living room and marched imperiously into her bedroom office, where she proceeded to open a file cabinet and pull out a stack of crumbling, bound scripts on onionskin paper. She said, "These have never been published. They have been just sitting there since the fifties, not doing anything. I want you to adapt these and produce them for me."

I was amazed to see the stack of plays, and asked her why she would ask me to do this. She said, "You are the only living playwright that I trust." And then gave me a very long hug. I began to adapt the scripts, have produced one play so far, *Love Letters of a Portuguese Nun,* and hope some day to see them filmed.

Madeleine and my father were good friends, and it disturbed her deeply when he was diagnosed with Alzheimer's. She prayed for him and always asked after him when I visited. Though she had various ailments in her later years, she was always very solicitous after the troubles of her friends. I will never forget visiting her after her stroke and hearing her say with absolute certainty that during the time she was in a coma, she was a whale swimming with a pod of whales singing whale song hymns. I fully believed her.

The most moving scene that played over and over in my mind as I lay in bed crying on the night I had the "Holy, Holy" dream was a memory of the last time I saw Madeleine. Her family had graciously told friends when she officially entered Hospice care, and I came to see her, as I had every summer, up in Goshen. I sat for several days at her bedside, quietly tapping on my laptop, praying, dozing, and occasionally getting up to get her something. She did not have very many words left, but used them all whenever possible. It was a very sacred time for me, full of grateful love, as every visit had ever been, but also full of tears, as I realized that this was my goodbye-for-now. When I could no longer delay my departure, amazingly, two other friends arrived to say their goodbyes, and as I gently kissed her forehead, and rose to try to memorize her face again, I could not quite leave yet, and leaned down one more time to kiss her. She looked up at me with a twinkly-but-grumpy look and said, "Enough." It was indeed time to go; she was making herself very clear about that.

Her memorial service up in Goshen was intimate and perfect, and it was a great blessing to be there with her generous family and friends, as I had been honored to be at several of her family's funerals in the past. On our way home, several of us stopped at favorite "Madeleine" spots: Dog Pond; the Goshen store and church; the road past Crosswicks and the Cottage. Then we met in a hotel room to say Compline and weep for her. She had been like a spiritual mother to all of us, and it was horribly, wonderfully right to pray together that night. Later there was another service in her beloved Cathedral, with all the pomp and circumstance that she adored, and that too was right.

Cornelia Duryée Moore and Madeleine, around 2004.

Last week another of Madeleine's godchildren wrote to me, saying, "I am missing Madeleine so much today! I just want to crawl onto the big four-poster bed together and pray Compline…" And I wrote her back, saying, "I ache like that most evenings. I probably always will."

Recently I woke from yet another dream of sitting next to Madeleine on the couch, after dinner, at Crosswicks. And she held my hand and said, "I know how much you love me." That has to be good enough for now. Because if I still believe everything that she taught me to believe, I trust that I will see her again.

Madeleine first taught me that I could have confidence in myself as a writer, and it is because of her that I am now a filmmaker. Though I often expressed my gratitude while she was here, those thanks will never be adequate. I hope that we can sit down together for a long visit after this life, so that I can take one eternity to thank her for each of her many great gifts to me, as she used to say about Bach. One for spiritual formation, one for introducing me to my husband, one for each career she inspired me to begin, on and on, celebrating, and then another eternity to just dance in worship with her.

This morning a third sacred dream came to me, and I have gotten up early to write it down, so early that the robins are singing their hymn to God, as they have on many important mornings in my life. I dreamed that Terry and I drove up one last time to Crosswicks to mourn Madeleine's death, as I did in real life two years ago with beloveds. In the dream we had been to a perfect dinner there the evening before, and had gotten word that she had died in the night, so we had driven over with our boys. We came in the Tower entrance to see the old wondrous, complicated kitchen still nearly the same as it had been when I used to stay there.

We glanced respectfully into the house, expecting to see a house of mourning, but what we saw was a kind woman trimming the hair of a lady in a cardigan and jeans, who looked like Madeleine. Then the lady got up to greet us—and it was Madeleine herself, alive and well. She welcomed us lovingly, as always, and then she began to show us around the house. It was much changed from the old days; the walls were more spare and glowing with light; many of her books had been stored, but those that were there were very important to her. I remember a book about Saint Godric on one shelf, and books about the healing properties of plants. She said she had new interests lately, and was thoroughly enjoying her new life. It was pure joy to see her so well. There were recent photos of her riding horses and driving boats, and many more delightful activities. She was brimming with energy and humor. And oh! to be in that house again, and exploring it with her. She was completely happy and at home again. Then somehow we exited the house through the third floor and were on a riverbank, where she got into a boat with other joyful people, waved lovingly, and as the boat left the shore, sailed into her next journey.

When we meet again, I hope indeed that she will show us around her new and (as she might say) "whole, hale, healthy, hearty, and holy" world. May it be so.

The grace our family sings over dinner, sung to the Tallis Canon, was one we sang with her:

Be present at this table, Lord
Be here, and everywhere, adored
These creatures bless, and grant that we
May feast in Paradise with Thee. Amen.

Madeleine L'Engle, Writer and Friend (1918–2007)

by Luci Shaw

Luci Shaw, a close friend of Madeleine's for more than thirty years, has published nearly thirty books, including ten poetry collections; Breath for the Bones: Art, Imagination and Spirit: Reflections on Creativity and Faith; *and* The Crime of Living Cautiously: Hearing God's Call to Adventure. *With Madeleine she authored* Friends for the Journey, *a book of essays and poems;* WinterSong, *a book of Christmas readings; and* A Prayer Book for Spiritual Friends. *As Senior Editor and later President at Shaw Publishers, Luci also edited a number of Madeleine's poetry volumes and reflective spiritual works, including* Walking on Water: Reflections on Art and Faith.

We were sitting in the old wicker chairs, having tea on the screened-in porch at Crosswicks Cottage, the second home built for Madeleine across the street from Crosswicks. It was a warm summer day in 2002, with the Litchfield Hills carving a silhouette against the late afternoon sky. Our conversation had slowed, become desultory, in the relaxed manner of friends who know from long experience how to be together, what the other person may be thinking, and for whom silence is comfortable, even comforting. I was knitting. Madeleine seemed preoccupied.

Suddenly she looked up and asked, "Is your journal there in your knitting bag?"

I answered, "Yes," rescuing my battered notebook from a tangle of yarn.

"Write this down for me, will you?"

Madeleine dictated this poem, speaking slowly enough for me to scribble it onto a blank page, but without a break in thought or rhythm.

> ...Purple shade
> Smudges the spill of light from the late day sun.
> The ink will run if I cannot remember
> To keep the darkness new—so easily forgot.

The night provides more light than blatant day.
What can I write that keeps the morning fresh
That hid the young cat in the row of wheat?

The reaper lacks the eyes to hold him back;
Unseeing, his sharp blade carves the damning cut
That kills without a conscious, caring thought.
He does not hear the harsh cry of the cat;
And spurting blood, and life gone like the wind.

The event of the poem was clearly a vivid memory, one that had long been at work in Madeleine's subconscious, ever-fruitful mind. It was as if the image finally found an outlet, and a place on a page.

Rereading this poem later, I kept discovering things. Like its human author, a good poem is layered, not revealed all at once.

For instance, the need to keep memory fresh and re-freshened by writing it down: "The ink will run/if I can not remember to keep the darkness new." Madeleine's personal journal and daybook, in which she wrote daily for most of her adult life, helped her to "keep the darkness new" and "the morning fresh" and guarded her ideas, and their sharp particularities, from blurring into mere abstractions. The long-ago stunning moment in its beauty and terror inform the poem as if it had just happened. The detail of "the young cat in the row of wheat" is stark and simple enough to paint a picture and prepare us for the violent conclusion of the second stanza.

Luci Shaw, Hugh, and Kristin Shaw at Crosswicks, 1982.

The contrast between light and darkness, and the paradoxical power of darkness to clarify the truth, to inform even through anguish and suffering, reminds us of the phrase Madeleine often quoted about "the deep but dazzling darkness" of God and of supernatural reality that we struggle to understand and enter.

The vast importance for Madeleine of clear vision, and of sight and insight, is emphasized by its utter absence in "the reaper" who "lacks the eyes to hold him back" from bloodshed, and because of indifference and lack of awareness, is unable to avoid snuffing out a life.

And "life gone like the wind"; in the age bracket where Madeleine and I found ourselves at the time, our mortality and the diminishment that comes with aging had to be faced. All of us who were close to Madeleine in her final months were painfully aware that her life seemed to be passing like the wind.

Madeleine has always had a powerful, instinctive sense of rhythm and rhyme. Try reading some of her sonnets aloud, and note how the flow of words and unforced, easy rhymes and rhythms sound as if they were always meant to sound that way. When read aloud, these poems, some deeply moving, some full of humor, come to life as if they had somewhere always existed in their present form and only needed a mind and a mouthpiece and a page to bring them to our attention.

Barbara Braver was a close friend of Madeleine's—her housemate part of each week for a dozen years during Barbara's time of commuting from Massachusetts to work in New York City. Through Madeleine, Barbara became my friend, and our companionship has grown with the years. Several years ago the three of us met in Ireland and then drove through Scotland and England together, from Iona, the Holy Island off the Scottish coast where St. Columba and his followers found sanctuary in exile, to Lindisfarne, the "Holy Island," and the Lake Country. Madeleine's ability spontaneously to speak poetry into existence made for a lot of fun as each of the three of us in turn would contribute a line or a stanza to an ongoing poem. Sometimes we'd get quite carried away into zany, pure buffoonery or raucous nonsense, especially in the limericks. Sometimes the verses made surprising, remarkable sense.

Madeleine L'Engle. What the world saw was a powerful woman, large-hearted, fearless, quixotic, profoundly imaginative, unwilling to settle for mediocrity. Tall and queenly, she physically embodied her mental and spiritual attributes. Some of us remember occasions when, in church during Advent, at her home church, All Angels' in Manhattan, she rose to full height, spread her arms wide like the Angel of the Annunciation, and declared, "Fear not!" in a tone that allowed no gainsaying. It was a challenge impossible to ignore.

She loved God and all his children, but this didn't keep her from questioning and questing in pursuit of truth, which she never equated with fact. Without ever being a scientist herself, she had an uncanny understanding of some of the principles of physics, and the thrust of her life was to integrate her sense of the largeness, diversity, and unity of the universe with the spiritual principles she found in Scripture, her wide reading, and her daily practice and rule of life.

We met in the seventies as speakers at a Wheaton College literary conference, exchanged books, affirmed each other as kindred spirits, and started a correspondence. Her reputation as a novelist and essayist was legendary, even then. *A Wrinkle in Time* had received the Newbery Medal, and the Crosswicks journals had just been published. Her first book of poetry, *Lines Scribbled on an Envelope*, had recently gone out of print, and since my husband Harold and I had recently started our publishing house, I asked her, "Why don't we reprint the volume in a new edition, along with some of your more recent poems?"

Madeleine jumped at the idea, and next year *The Weather of the Heart* was released and, later, newer poems in *A Cry Like a Bell*. Madeleine welcomed my suggestions for minor revisions to her poems (and, tit for tat, was never reticent to comment constructively on mine, as in "You don't need that last line; it's redundant"). As we worked together it became abundantly clear to me that this woman had a lot to say to our particular, somewhat restricted circles of Christian community.

Walking on Water, Madeleine's work on the complex, mysterious connections between faith and art, came about early in our relationship. After the publication of her poetry, I asked her to write a book for Shaw Publishers about her philosophy of creativity. In a couple of months she handed me an untidy bundle of typescript, saying with some disgust, "Can you *do something* with this? It has *no shape!*" After weeks of cutting the whole thing apart and re-organizing it on my dining room floor (this predated computers) I presented it to her. She was relieved, excited that it worked. Her husband, Hugh, loved it. It became *Walking on Water: Reflections on Art and Faith*, a book that has been reprinted many times and continues to encourage artists of faith around the globe.

After that I became editor and publisher of her "non-secular" books. As we all know, Madeleine loved to jolt her readers out of their conventional ruts, gaining their attention by presenting radical ideas. Her fresh insights set us all thinking in new and fruitful ways, opening up new horizons.

Of course, as we worked through manuscripts we often had disagreements. As her editor, I wanted her books to command the widest attention and truly represent her fresh thoughts and ideas without unduly provoking those with divergent convictions. I'd complain that some expression or perspective might raise a red flag for some readers ("Madeleine, you can't say that!"), upon which Madeleine would demonstrate why it was her intention to say exactly that. We never actually fought, but we regularly entered into vigorous differences of opinion. Sometimes one of us would win, sometimes the other, but we both considered our differing viewpoints as a great advantage in our friendship, growing as it did out of a working editorial bond.

We learned astonishing things from being honest and forthright with each other, "as iron sharpens iron." Coming as we did from opposite ends of the Christian spectrum, we nearly always met in the middle, benefiting from rich interchanges and discussions. "Book talk and God talk" formed continuing themes in our letters, phone conversations, manuscript revisions, and face-to-face conversations. I remember our standing up and singing the Doxology when a particularly tricky conflict had been resolved.

Madeleine completed a number of "meditative" books for Shaw, including *The Genesis Trilogy*, *The Rock That Is Higher*, *Penguins and Golden Calves*, and *Bright Evening Star*, all with Scriptural themes. She knew her Bible more thoroughly and perceptively than many Evangelicals. Scripture was very much part of her daily life and thought.

Our friendship blossomed way beyond the writer-editor relationship. There were the lectures we gave together at Regent College, Calvin College, and at Oxford and Cambridge. There were wonderful parties at "924," her home in Manhattan, her famous roast leg of lamb dinners, and proofreading sessions on her dining room table, supervised by Terrible and Kelly, the literary cats. There was all the mutual support given in times of crisis, such as the year both our husbands died of cancer, or when I was depressed enough to be near-suicidal, and Madeleine talked me down, like talking the pilot of a failed plane to a safe landing. After she'd been badly injured in a car crash and hospitalized with serious internal injuries, I was able to be with her in San Diego for a week of telling jokes and singing hymns and telling bedtime stories as she healed.

Our pursuits together were never only theological or literary. There were Scrabble games. There were the ping-pong tournaments at Laity Lodge in Texas, where we led some retreats together. Madeleine was a skilled player who sometimes won by pure intimidation, bearing down on any helpless opponent like a ship under full sail. (I wanted to title our book on friendship *The Table of Friendship,* celebrating Madeleine's dinner table, the Lord's Table, the editorial desk, and the ping-pong table. Madeleine thought that sounded too much like the multiplication table, to which we were both averse. So it ended up as *Friends for the Journey*, aided and abetted and immeasurably encouraged by Barbara.)

Luci Shaw and Madeleine, Oxford, 1999 (top) and 1994 (bottom).

There were evenings together in the Texas hill country (unhindered in that remote area by any ambient light in the sky), marveling at the magnitude of the universe and space from this "star-watching place."

There were public dialogues, unplanned conversations that could lead us into territory where we had to think on our feet, knowing that if one of us went blank or dropped the ball the other would pick it up. We loved the adventure of Q and A, where candor led us to ad-lib responses, sometimes voicing things we never knew we knew. We were profoundly aware that we were both servants of the word, and the Word.

One such occasion was in Oxford, at the Sheldonian Theatre, Christopher Wren's marvelous U-shaped auditorium. Two upholstered wing chairs were set up on the stage with an elegant Victorian tea table and a pot of hot tea and scones between them. We sat back comfortably and talked about the deep need for friendship in our current culture, and our friendship in particular, batting the subject back and forth like a tennis ball, teasing, getting serious, telling stories, answering questions. When there's enough that is the same and enough that is different in such a relationship, there is a large middle ground to be explored.

Because of the success of her Newbery Award-winning novel, *A Wrinkle in Time*, and the popular fiction series that followed, as well as her more contemplative nonfiction books, Madeleine's readership was vast and vocal. Her ideas seemed to ring a bell in so many readers' thinking and discovery of life and its values. She had to deal with the struggle that numbers of public figures face, where everyone wanted a piece of her, wanted to own part of her. She was always gracious and giving, sometimes signing books for a long line of fans until her hand actually bled, but she admitted to me, "I am really grateful to be so loved, but I don't want to be *adored*."

It didn't take long for me to come to truly love her. Raised in the most conservative of circles—British, male-dominated, genteel, and fundamentalist—I was always the questioner, the challenger, the seeker within my group. As a woman, I was considered out of order if I raised my voice in worship services or asked questions, which were to be submitted in private to my husband. At the time I was speaking and writing to Christian groups around the country which signified, to those in my own circle, that I was a "trouble-maker." The radical in me met the feisty, openhearted, broad-minded Episcopalian in Madeleine, and the mix was warming and enriching for us both. When my husband and I finally joined the Episcopal Church, Madeleine welcomed us with happy enthusiasm. We converged in the middle and from then on, I believe, influenced each other's understandings of our mysterious life with God.

Madeleine was uncomfortable with the doctrine of substitutionary atonement. For her, the idea that Jesus had to be punished by his Father for human beings to be forgiven signified what she called a "forensic" understanding of theology. "How could a loving God ever kill his Beloved Son?" she would ask. In the continuum of God's Love and Righteousness she came down squarely on the Love end of things. She also prayed that eventually "every knee will bow" to God, not just in submission but in adoration, that "no-one will finally be excluded from the party." She hoped that "no human being's rebellion could outlive the love of God," brought to this hope by her reading of George MacDonald's theology. We discussed this endlessly, for my part referencing C. S. Lewis' depiction of MacDonald in *The Great Divorce* that ran counter to her conviction. I guess I came to think: "Well, if universalism is a heresy, it's one I wish were true!"

Inevitably she came under attack from conservatives for her views. *Trojan Horse: How the New Age Movement Infiltrates the Church*, a book that was presented at the Christian Booksellers Association Convention back in the seventies, claimed that Madeleine was the thin edge of heterodoxy seeping through the armor of orthodoxy. She responded with such a sweet spirit, disclaiming the traditionalist stereotype of her as a "New Ager," and refusing to respond in kind to her assailants so that they had nowhere to go. Her feeling was that her detractors were drawing a circle that was exclusionary, while Jesus' circle drew her in. I never stopped feeling that we were in that circle together. The love of Christ bonded us.

In 1998, in honor of her eightieth birthday, Shaw Publishers issued a *festschrift* titled *The Swiftly Tilting Worlds of Madeleine L'Engle,* with sixteen essays by friends and admirers including Thomas Cahill, Katherine Paterson, Eugene Peterson, Walter Wangerin, Jr., and Walter Wink. Many of us gathered for a festive event at Wheaton College and completely surprised Madeleine. It was only one of a multitude of honors she received during her lifetime.

Her birthday was November 29, exactly a month before my December birth date. We'd try to celebrate one or other of these birthdays together. Once when the date was approaching I asked Madeleine, "What would you like for your birthday?" To which she shot back immediately, "Go on a trip with me." We drove together through the Canadian Rockies, in awe at their vastness and beauty. We stayed at some glorious hotels in Banff and Jasper and made up for our extravagance with some cheap B & Bs.

Then there was our trip to Ireland, England, and Scotland with Barbara Braver. As I drove on some of the narrow country lanes of the U.K., hedgerows almost brushing the car on either side, Madeleine, sitting on the right next to

Punting in Oxford, 1998, with Luci Shaw and Luci's husband, John Hoyte.

me as we drove along the "left" of the road, would often urge me, "More left-ish, Luci. More left-ish." "But Madeleine, I'm as far left as I can go! And as far right, too." This pretty much summed up, metaphorically, our being drawn together to the centrality of our belief in God and of the Way of Christ, his "strait and narrow," if you will.

As wordsmiths, Madeleine and I both loved to trace words back to their derivations. The etymological dictionary in her study gave us one of our most enjoyable ways of working with language and verbal expressions. We'd both learned other languages when we were in school—French for Madeleine, Latin and Greek for me. We realized that "astonishment" is related to the word for thunder. That "cataract" is about something breaking down—either the tissue of the cornea, or a river flowing over a cliff. When the word "companion" came under scrutiny we realized that it referred to those who ate bread together. (She observed that when feuding countries forged some kind of peace accord and shook hands for the cameras, it didn't mean much. But if they sat down to a meal together, with bread and salt, it spoke of something more profound.) The Lord's Table, with Eucharistic bread and wine, was the feast that joined us together. When I visited New York City we regularly walked to noon Eucharist at the Cathedral of St. John the Divine, a few blocks from Madeleine's home, and then had lunch together at a restaurant across Amsterdam Avenue, followed by a visit to the office she worked in, as Cathedral Librarian, in the cathedral close. If the weather was too severe we'd stay indoors, thankful for God's presence in the fellowship of tuna salad sandwiches.

WinterSong, our first book compiled together, mingled our poems, essays, stories, and journal entries that reflected light into the dark period of the year. Because we found praying together on the phone so helpful and meaningful, we then assembled *A Prayer Book for Spiritual Friends*, a collection of prayers "in two voices" that friends can pray together about themes of common interest, such as forgiveness, doubt, or how to help a friend. Often our prayers together over the phone spanned the gulf of time and space as East and West coasts met each other in God's presence. Finally came *Friends for the Journey*, celebrating our commitment of friend with friend over many years. We called this a "Trinitarian" friendship book, reflecting the way our three-way friendship with Barbara, our fellow pilgrim in travels and in faith, had enriched all our lives.

Friendships for Madeleine were never just "relationships" or networking opportunities, but companionships of heart and mind and spirit. That's what her fans and readers can continue to celebrate, by loving each other and remembering the luminous moments with our loving, faithful friend or her books.

Many of her close friends grieved for months, years, as she was slipping away into another sphere. I wrote this prayer-poem shortly after my last visit with her in November 2006. Barbara Braver and I had driven to Litchfield and the nursing home where she was being lovingly cared for before she died. She did not know us. That was so hard. Though we sang hymns and prayed with her, there was no visible response. Heartbreaking.

Path to the Edge

for Madeleine L'Engle, November, 2006

Be with her now. She faces the ocean
of unknowing, losing the sense
of what her life has been, and soon

will be no longer as she knew it, as
we knew it with her. Far behind,
we cannot join her on this nameless shore.

Knots in her bones, flesh flaccid, the skin
like paper, pigment gathering like ashes driven
by a random wind, a heart

that may still sing, interiorly—we cannot
know—have pulled her far ahead of us,
our pioneer.

As we embrace her, her inner eyes embrace
the universe. She recognizes heaven with its
innumerable stars—but not our faces.

Be with her now, as you have
sometimes been—a flare that blazes,
then dulls, leaving only a bright

blur in the memory. Hold her
in the mystery that no one can describe
but Lazarus, though he was dumb

and didn't speak of it. Fog has rolled in,
erasing definition at the edge. Walking
to meet it, she hopes soon to see

where the shore ends. She listens as
the ocean breathes in and out in waves.
She hears no other sound.

Madeleine's legacy is with us in her books, our memories, her friends, and ours—an immense cloud of witnesses. We keep her alive in our hearts, our God-friend, as she is now "knowing as she was known," by her heavenly Father.

Madeleine and Luci Shaw, proofreading at 924 West End Avenue, 1994; notice cat Tatiana.

The Journey to Becoming

by Barbara Braver

Barbara Braver met Madeleine when assigned by a magazine to do a profile of her in 1985. Barbara is a writer and editor who edited a book co-authored by Madeleine and Luci Shaw, Friends for the Journey. *For a dozen years, Barbara shared Madeleine's New York apartment for part of each week.*

It would be interesting to know how many writers' workshops Madeleine L'Engle conducted over the years—how many volumes of words she coaxed forth from both seasoned and aspiring writers. Year after year new groups met with her—in university classrooms, in parish halls, at retreat centers, and in her own comfortable living room. I have no idea of their number, and I suspect Madeleine would not have known herself. This I do know: Madeleine's own writing, and her teaching about writing, encouraged and nurtured other writers struggling to put pen to paper, fingers to keyboard.

Before they met Madeleine, many thought of themselves merely as scribbling in secret, possibly to no good purpose. Then, they drank thirstily from her well, and discovered they had stories waiting to be told. With her encouragement they began to believe in their own work. And they were cheered on by Madeleine's own wisdom on the topic. "I am not meant to be Shakespeare. I am meant to be Madeleine," she firmly declared, thus giving others permission to be themselves, too.

Some of her students knew their teacher only from her writings. Even from a distance, her influence could be formative, and formidable. "She is my mentor. I keep her picture next to my computer," said a St. Louis woman I once met who had been inspired and encouraged by *Walking on Water,* a book of reflections on faith and art that reflects the quintessential Madeleine as teacher of the craft, discipline, and mystery of writing.

Though Madeleine's almost intuitive articulation of the creative process was a gift to her students, so too was her model of unselfconsciousness once the pen gets going. "When the work takes over, then the artist is enabled to get out of the way, not to interfere. When the work takes over, then the artist listens," she wrote.

So, the thinking comes before the writing. And, for Madeleine, it would happen like this. One minute she was with me in her kitchen, we were talking away about whatever most engaged either or both of us at the moment, and all the while she was vigorously chopping cloves of garlic on a wooden board, creating a fabulous sauce for pasta. The next minute, the only sound was the knife on the board and Madeleine was miles away, perhaps communing with her characters, who might be on a journey beyond the stars. Her mind was in another place: thinking.

Then, each day, every day, she allowed the work to take over and she listened, sitting silent with her yellow pad on her lap, or coming, faithful, to the computer as if to a romantic rendezvous. She listened, got out of the way, and the words came. And after, after the writing, she spent concentrated hours revising her manuscripts with precise, calligraphic markings.

Madeleine offered a marvelous gift in her description of the fearsome act of letting go to creativity and "riding the wind," as she called it. Her joyful free flights have emboldened others to let go and to follow. Through generous offerings of herself, Madeleine went far beyond imparting the rules of her craft. At a deeper level, she has been—and is still through her writing and our memories—a companion and fellow pilgrim, willing to walk with you as you do the hard work of stringing one word after another, telling stories, making meaning, and most of all, becoming your truest self, the person God intends you to become.

To my joy, Madeleine and I traveled together for many years on the road to becoming. We first met in the mid-1980s when I took on an assignment from a magazine to write a profile of her. I took a picture of her on that occasion, relaxed, smiling, open to the moment. Of course, I have it still. Over the next years we visited as we could, corresponded regularly and kept, as she called it, "in telephonic communication." Several years into our friendship I grabbed a fabulous opportunity to do work I loved, fabulous except for the depressing reality that doing this work meant I had to leave home and husband and spend several nights each week in New York City. Frequent dinners with Madeleine were a happy compensation.

When her granddaughters, who had delighted her by living in her spacious apartment with her during their grad school days, moved on into new chapters, Madeleine invited me to be her "housemate." I accepted with alacrity and there I remained for some dozen years, a time of grace and delight as we shared a great deal of laughter and some tears, prayed together, and generally enjoyed the extraordinary blessings, ever available, in the seemingly ordinary events of our lives.

Looking back on it now I am most especially grateful for Madeleine's quiet nurture of my own creative spark and her understanding of the writing struggles that have been part of my consciousness for my whole life. When I was a wee girl of ten I started a newspaper called *Neighborhood News.* The only major story I remember was a cat funeral, but then not much happened in the semi-rural community of my growing-up days. The paper lasted for several months, coming out weekly. I wrote the copy and laboriously pecked it out on Uncle Jim's ancient Underwood, the kind with round keys, black inside, the letter in white and a silver rim. It probably wasn't all that old at the time. My collaborator and chum, Susan Stanley, and I went door to door with our few copies, each originally typed. (Who knew about photocopies?)

My next memorable experience of the writing life was the year I moved into the teen age, the big thirteen. My friend Martha Taylor and I would regularly creep out of our respective houses at sunrise on summer mornings in search of dewy grass and poetic inspiration. Martha's dog usually trailed along, and the line I still remember was inspired by this solid little furry companion: "Bucky is my dog, my own." (In the poem, I changed his name from Zachary because I thought it was important to preserve his anonymity when I became famous.)

In spite of such writing proclivities, and my formal education in English and journalism, I didn't easily come to name myself a writer. Except for babysitting here and there and my brief and totally unmemorable career in the tie department at Kaufmann's Department Store in Pittsburgh, Pennsylvania, during my college years, I have never made a cent for doing anything except writing or editing in one form or another. Even so, writers were not people like me, and certainly not specifically me: they were Shakespeare, or Milton, or Blake or Louisa May Alcott or Flannery O'Connor or Willa Cather. It is from personal experience that I witness to Madeleine's ministry of encouragement, and her coaxing forth of words.

So, here comes my "mouse in the wall theory." *If you see one, you have lots.* So, I write now as one representative of the great many grateful souls to whom Madeleine provided the necessary courage to let go and ride the wind.

In these next pages I offer poems of *becoming.* I have included among them a few sonnets because that form was important to Madeleine from the time of her teen years when she began to write sonnets. Within the strict form, she found freedom. In *A Circle of Quiet* she describes the sonnet as "the perfect analogy of the structure which liberates."

My own sense is that the sonnet form not only provides a discipline within which to be free, but that in working out the rhyme, I find what is true for me and uncover feelings previously unavailable to me in my conscious mind. In *A Wrinkle in Time,* one of Madeleine's wise characters, Mrs Whatsit, compares our lives to a sonnet: a strict form, but with freedom within it. As Mrs Whatsit says:

"You're given the form, but you have to write the sonnet yourself. What you say is completely up to you." And, isn't it so for writers, to our fear and unspeakable delight: "What you say is completely up to you."

This offering of sonnets and other poems of becoming are interspersed with Madeleine's own words from *Walking on Water,* Shaw, 1980.

> "When the work takes over, then the artist is enabled to get out of the way, not to interfere. When the work takes over, then the artist listens. But before he can listen, paradoxically, he must work."

Inspiration

It serves the work to halt my searching flight,
the restless circling of the outer quest,
and thus find what is seen with inner sight,
when body, mind, and spirit come to rest.

But quietness is not my usual way,
and lesser cares have fouled my inner place,
as louder voices hold soft ones at bay
and weeds choke off my path to sacred space.

My task is first to tug out every weed,
to silence errant voices that intrude,
eliminate those forces that impede,
and wait on Spirit-muse like lover wooed.

And when I have enacted my small part,
I wait for gifts of words to fill my heart.

> "An artist at work is in a condition of complete and total faith."

No poetry

For days, weeks, no poetry.
No message wells up
from my truest being.

Perhaps I have not gone down,
to meet her
        in the soul place.

Have I merely greeted her in passing
an acquaintance
        worthy of a careless wave?

Or is she the current patient
on my examining table
to whom I give focused attention
        over a narrow range?

No meetings these.
How then, to meet her?

Since you ask, she will show you:
in the terrors of the night
in the beauty of the morning;
in bread broken, where she is at-one
with all that is,
        seen and unseen.

Find her thus.
Attend to the moment,
        full of grace.
Strike the rock
        and watch the water gush forth,
        living.

"As I run over my favorite characters in both Old and new Testaments, I can't find one who was in any worldly way qualified to do the job which was nevertheless accomplished."

The Sabbatical Sonnets

I. Sabbatical

The pages tempt me with their unmarked space
these summer months when I can simply be
and wonder through the wilds of inner place
allowing soul and body to float free.

Still I must look for guides along the way
some bread crumbs on the path to finding me
or into brambles and dark voids I'll stray
    and from the pregnant silence I might flee.

This time of God's is given as a gift
and God will cast those crumbs for me to find
God's purpose will emerge through focused drift
as false bonds loosen and the truer bind.

I say good-bye for now to safe routine
to search in faith for futures dimly seen.

II. The reckoning

I sing a song of summer that has fled
and find my song begins as a lament
for hours and days that from my store were bled
for time now gone and possibly misspent.

As fall returns so does the inner court
to stand in judgment on my use of time
They say that they can give no good report
on fits and starts and efforts worth one dime.

Stand down, I shout. Stand down. You are dismissed.
You have no sense of who or what I am.
Your judgments I will consciously resist
and for your views I do not give a damn.

This holy time was God's own gift to me.
Of my return we'll have to wait and see.

III. The resolution

Were I to take a measure of these days
I'd ask myself about my faithfulness.
I'd ponder if I've found some truer way
and tended to God's leading, more or less.

Am I now more who I am meant to be?
Have I made progress on the pilgrim's road?
Can I some further growth expect to see
from bulbs I planted and from seeds I sowed?

I dare to ask these questions, then I wait
for I myself the answers do not know.
As only God's own Spirit knows my fate,
I pray that towards God's vision I might grow.

Content for now to be a lump of clay
as in the potter's loving hands I stay.

"Because I am a story teller, I live by words…Stories are able to help us become more whole, to become named."

The words inside me

The words inside me
bump against each other
and abrade my soft interior.

They gather,
a teasing chorus,
pose mute,
and then
at some secret signal
hurl themselves
against the drawn curtain
of my consciousness.

By day,
they drop,
insensible,
and litter my unplowed field
like so many cowpies
carelessly dropped
until walking is dangerous.

At night,
I awaken to their frolic,
too late,
and watch them go
leaving only silvery trails,
evanescent.

At first light,
I open wide
to let them out
and they vaporize
against a still background
to gather strength
for another rush.

I've come to know them now
and so will lay my plan
that they might stay
tamed, somewhat,
and sign,
at least,
my guest book.

Barbara Braver, Luci Shaw, and Madeleine, just outside London, August 1998.

Barbara Braver and Madeleine, Iona, 1996.

The Inventory

When King Henry died,
a scant 55 years—
though who would believe it
given his marital history,
and the swells and creases
of his swollen girth—
a commission was appointed
to measure, count, and catalogue
his worldly goods,
from the crown that weighted his regal head
to the collar that fit round the neck
of his favorite hound.

The inventory of his possessions
fills four substantial volumes
kept for historians
and the merely curious
at the British Museum:
the material history of a life
in small detail,
the worn pillows, frayed curtains,
cutlery, cups and clothing,
and one mottled leather eyeglass case,
the detritus of his earthly days.

And what of me, at a greater age,
my accumulations, accretions?
When I die, who will count each pillow
and note its wear?
The attic horde could fill one book,
things left behind, at each chapter's end:
a button-eyed doll,
yellowing silks of baptisms
and a wedding
skates grown dull
boots now porous

letters crumbling
and broken chairs,
rump-sprung.
What could they tell of me,
and my mortal life?

Little enough,
I think,
and some misleading traces:
I have not saved with thoughts of history.

Better to find a living witness
who remembers laughter
wrote down stories
noted sins, and counted blessings
remarked on warm hands
measured longing, and joy
one who knew me
as I was.

Better to find a true witness
and leave my possessions,
unnumbered, unrecorded,
trusting,
rather,
in a living word.

There are many true witnesses to who Madeleine was and to who she was becoming. I am grateful to be one such witness, and to provide a living word.

Love, God, Faith, Risk and How I Became Madeleine L'Engle's Nineteenth Godchild

by Sandy Hudson

Sandy Hudson was a close friend of Madeleine's who attended her writers' workshops and retreats in monasteries, convents, colleges, and retreat centers in New York, Connecticut, Illinois, and North Carolina for over fifteen years. She operates a small chauffeuring business in Indiana.

I first became aware of Madeleine L'Engle in 1968 when I was a junior in college and took children's literature, a requirement for my B. S. in elementary education. *A Wrinkle in Time* was one of the one hundred books we had to read. Thereafter I would occasionally peruse the "L" shelf in the children's section of the local library, and if Madeleine had written a new book, I'd check it out. In the mid-seventies a librarian friend told me that Madeleine also wrote books for adults, so I checked out *A Circle of Quiet*. The first year I was married (1979), when my husband, Andy, asked me what I wanted for Christmas, I asked for (and received) my own copy of *A Wrinkle in Time*.

On December 6, 1983, I read in the Indianapolis newspaper that Madeleine L'Engle would be giving a public talk *that* night—just a few blocks from our home. I went, but recalled little of what she said because I spent the whole time thinking, "Oh, my God, that's Madeleine L'Engle!" Afterward she autographed my copy of *Wrinkle* and I rudely took her picture without asking.

Early in 1984 I took another class in children's literature and ordered a subscription to *Horn Book Magazine*. While waiting for hours in an allergist's office, I read my first issue and was stunned to find a copy of a speech Madeleine had delivered at Simmons College, "Do I Dare Disturb the Universe?" Parts of the speech seemed vaguely familiar as it contained elements of her talk in Indianapolis. I thought my heart was going to explode ... Madeleine discussed so many things I'd been thinking and wondering about—love, God, faith, risk.

One of the assignments for the children's literature class was to write a paper explaining why one author's body of work was important to the field. The instructor said, "No problem!" when I told him my choice, Madeleine L'Engle. I reread five of her "children's" books and *A Circle of Quiet.* In the latter, when I read "I was looking in the wrong mirrors," I thought, "I think I'm in love." Those seven words changed my life.

Meanwhile, I had written Madeleine, sent her a copy of her photo, and was ecstatic when she replied. My paper about her, "Timeless and Timely," received an A, so I wrote again and sent her a copy. As I was typing, the Holy Spirit must surely have taken over, because I found myself asking if my husband and I were to visit NYC in the spring, could we take her out to lunch? Would she be my birthday present? Madeleine wrote back and said YES! and included the phone number of the library at St. John the Divine. She asked that I call her. Never before or since have I been so nervous; I could not believe it when she herself answered the phone. We arranged to meet on May 16, 1984, when she was coming back to the city from Goshen, Connecticut, to speak to a women's group at the Cathedral.

When Madeleine and Hugh arrived at the Cathedral, she needed to use the ladies' room, which I badly needed, but hadn't been able to find. So within minutes of meeting the person I'd idolized for sixteen years, we were sharing the same bathroom. While in the stalls, Madeleine told me she'd recently commandeered an empty men's room during intermission at the symphony, because the ladies' room was so crowded. Since then, I've used a men's room several times when the ladies' room was full.

Madeleine showed Andy and me around the Cathedral before we walked across the street for lunch. Once I sat down, it hit me: "Oh, my God, that's Madeleine L'Engle sitting across from me!" It felt as if my brain had blown a fuse. I was literally speechless for a few minutes, but I recovered. When the bread came, Madeleine poked the soft center out and ate only the hard crust. I thought that was so New York, so citified and sophisticated, so weird. (Years later, when she did the same thing at a meal, I told her about my first response to seeing her do that. She laughed and explained that she simply preferred the crust.)

Walking back to the Cathedral library after lunch, we met a bald-headed man with a golden retriever. I knew it had to be Edward West, aka "Canon Tallis." He joined us in the library, and I still cherish my photos of Madeleine and him with their sibling goldens.

I had prepared some questions I wanted to ask Madeleine, which she graciously answered. Then I accompanied her to the women's group, listened in rapt attention as she spoke, and eventually tore myself away when Hugh returned to

Madeleine and Sandy Hudson.

Madeleine at 924 West End Avenue, 1993.

drive her back to the country. As Andy and I pulled away from the Cathedral in a cab, I remember thinking, "I'm going to see her again."

Indeed, I was blessed to see Madeleine again and again and again over the next twenty years. I attended her writers' workshops and retreats in monasteries, convents, colleges, and retreat centers in New York, Connecticut, Illinois, and North Carolina, meeting so many people who are still among my very dearest friends. Along the way, Madeleine and I also became friends; I was honored to be a guest in her New York apartment, Crosswicks, and Crosswicks Cottage in Connecticut many times and to have her as a guest in my home three times; to meet her kids, grandkids, two cousins, and some of her personal friends; to attend worship with her at St. John's, All Angels', the Congregational Church in Goshen, and my church in Indianapolis. She used parts of conversations we'd had in three books and mentioned me by name in one.

When Madeleine appeared at a big gathering in Indianapolis, she introduced me as her goddaughter to several of the speakers and organizers. A few months later, as Madeleine and I walked with her dog along a country road in Connecticut, I shared how special I had felt when she called me her goddaughter. Her response was, "We should make it official." And a few months later, at Holy Cross Monastery in West Park, New York, where I most frequently attended Madeleine's workshops, we did just that. One of the monks adapted the wedding service for us, and during the Sunday morning worship service, I became Madeleine L'Engle's nineteenth godchild.

When my daughter was born less than two months after the first time I attended Holy Cross (in January 1985), I named her Katharine Saranam. Katharine is for Katharine Hepburn, whose independence and uniqueness I had always admired; Saranam is a Sanskrit word in Madeleine's book *A House Like a Lotus,* which says it means refuge and that refuge is God's richest blessing. I decided *Saranam* could mean God's richest blessing, which Katie (now twenty-four) surely is.

As I write this piece, it's been slightly over a year since Madeleine died. Two days ago she would have been ninety. Next to Katie, Madeleine affected me and the direction of my life more than anyone. She taught me about God's adoption and grace and made me the recipient of her own. I will love her, be down-on-my-knees grateful to God for her, and miss her forever.

Madeleine at the Melrose Convent, 1980s.

Everything I Need to Know I Learned from Madeleine L'Engle

by Sandy Hudson

I was looking in the wrong mirrors. Equal and like aren't the same thing. We are all called to be co-creators with God. Both/and, not either/or. I matter! Love is not a feeling, it's what you do.

If the ladies' room is full and the men's room is empty, stage a coup. To accept your gift means accepting your freedom. Grief is a part of life and you have to go through it.

The important thing is that God made everything, not when or how. We don't always have to know why. I believe … even when I don't. Faith should be fluid. I am all the ages I have ever been.

God made us all, loves us all, and wants us all to come back home. Long, laugh-filled, candle-lit dinners with good friends of all ages are a foretaste of the heavenly banquet.

Even prayers that seem to go unanswered help. All shall be well, and all shall be well, and all manner of thing shall be well — Lady Julian of Norwich. Good art is incarnational. Life's too short to read bad books.

Use a plastic bag to pick up dog poop; at night, don't fold it over and no one will bother you. A hero is a frame of reference. I'm free, not independent. Our view of God affects our view of everything.

He Will Raise You Up On Eagle's Wings. The Jesus Prayer. The daily offices, especially Compline. Saint Patrick's Breastplate. Surely the Presence of the Lord Is in This Place.

My heart, soul, body, and faith belong in the Episcopal Church. The more you love, the more vulnerable you are … and it's worth it. We find what we look for. Structure liberates. I can love a dog.

Holy Cross Monastery   Ellis Peters   Pachelbel's Canon   Bach everything   Hyfrydol melody   Tallis Canon   George MacDonald   The Community of the Holy Spirit

The opposite of love isn't hate, it's indifference. Water served in silver goblets is elegant. Maybe Jesus cursed the fig tree because he was tired and frustrated. Fear not! Jesus chose love over law.

The Bible is too serious to be taken literally. If Jesus was exactly like me except without sin, then he wasn't exactly like me. We are Christians because someone told us the story. Sin is separation from God.

Comparisons are odious. It's okay to be mad at God; you can't be mad at someone who isn't there. Perfect means thorough. Etymology can change your life. Icons are a window to God.

Not having to unlearn about God is a blessing. Forgiveness is not a do-it-yourself activity; I have to be willing to let God help me forgive. Being called to be a light bearer is the most wonderful vocation of all.

Chronos vs. *Kairos*   Ananda   Ontology   Circadian   Paradox   Curing vs. healing   Contradiction   Oblation   Eschatology   Kythe   Truth vs. fact

Crème brûlée, pesto, couscous, and lamb are delicious. When I am judgmental about judgmental people, I'm being just like them. Salad makes a good dessert. Jesus didn't heal or save or convert everyone.

God goes to great lengths to choose the unqualified. I can have a personal relationship with God. In prayer and writing, inspiration comes after starting, not before. Anger keeps fear and sorrow at bay.

If you've been hurt and press that emotional bruise and it doesn't hurt, you've forgiven. If Mary had been full of reason, there would have been no room for the child.

Questions are more important than answers. We are most ourselves when we are unselfconscious. Praying keeps my mind from useless wandering. My faults can be blessings.

God's glory is manifest when we love each other. Really knowing myself keeps me from hating others. Calling someone by name is an act of community. Christmas cards postmarked by January 6 aren't late.

When I can pray, "Thy will be done, no matter what," I have truly let go of the results. God's love can't be understood, only affirmed. Praying, like playing the piano and writing, takes practice.

Authors have to be firmly grounded in God's love to explore the darkest regions of the heart. God does not cause bad things to happen to teach us, but we can let God teach us when bad things happen.

It's God's table; who are we to think we're in charge of the guest list? Father incomprehensible, Son incomprehensible, Holy Ghost incomprehensible, whole damn thing incomprehensible.

Refuge is God's richest blessing; safety was never part of the promise. We are all children of God by adoption and grace. It is quite something to love and be loved by Madeleine L'Engle.

Dare to disturb the universe!

The Narrative Art of Madeleine L'Engle

by Carole F. Chase

Carole F. Chase, a retired Presbyterian minister, was a professor of religious studies at Elon University in North Carolina from 1976–2001. During that time, she developed a course called "Religious Dimensions of the Writings of Madeleine L'Engle." A friend of Madeleine for two decades, she wrote Suncatcher: A Study of Madeleine L'Engle and Her Writing *and compiled two books of Madeleine's works,* Glimpses of Grace *and* Madeleine L'Engle Herself.

In January 1984, I took a sabbatical from my university teaching position to study feminist ethics and theology. I was doing just that, immersing myself in the writings of Mary Daly, Beverly Harrison, Rosemary Ruether, Anne Wilson Schaef, Elizabeth Dodson Gray, Letty Russell, and others, when I happened to pick up, for pleasure reading, a young adult novel titled *A Ring of Endless Light.* As I read the book, I fell under the spell of a storyteller named Madeleine L'Engle. Since then, I have been on a journey to understand this woman, her stories, and myself.

Madeleine and Carole Chase in Elon, North Carolina, around 1989.

I had been familiar with Madeleine's writing for about ten years and had read her well-known Newbery Medal winner, *A Wrinkle in Time,* and its companion, *A Wind in the Door,* as well as two nonfiction books in the *Crosswicks Journal* series, *A Circle of Quiet* and *The Irrational Season.* So why did her writing have this impact on me in January 1984?

It was because this fiction story for young adults contained almost all the characteristics, concerns, and themes of feminist theology and feminist ethics that I had been reading about in my more academic and technical books. They were presented in the most straightforward, natural, and unapologetic way. The protagonist in *Ring of Endless Light* was a teenager and a girl. The story made it clear that one should be concerned for the environment as a friend to be cared for and not as an object to be exploited. While reason was not disparaged, it was taken for granted that intuition and subjectivity were equally valid as vehicles for perceiving reality. As I read *Ring of Endless Light* with a mind filled with scholarly arguments and six-syllable words, I discovered the lovely incarnation of the goals of feminism in a fiction book marketed for young adults.

A Severed Wasp had just been published, and I read that next with great anticipation. Madeleine did not disappoint me. This is an adult novel whose chief protagonist is Katherine Vigneras, a retired concert pianist who has returned to New York City to live. Her friendship with Mimi Oppenheimer, an orthopedic surgeon, provides the reader with a statement about friendships between women. At one point in the story, wise Katherine, who reminds me so much of Madeleine, advises troubled Dorcas Gibson that she can be both a dancer and a wife and mother.

In the feminist writing of academia, it is assumed that women are not being treated equally but they ought to be, and carefully wrought arguments are made, not always gently, for women's place in our society and in our churches to be equal to that of men. I realized that what Madeleine L'Engle had been doing for decades in her stories was writing about a world where it is natural to assume, among other things, that women are equal to men in talents, opportunities, and importance.

Then I remembered other L'Engle novels I had read. Mrs. Murry, Meg's mother in *A Wrinkle in Time* and the other books in L'Engle's time series, is really *Dr.* Murry. She has two Ph.D.'s in science and has won the Nobel Prize. These pieces of information about Mrs. Murry are presented in as matter-of-fact a way as possible. There are no *ohs* or *ahs* of surprise. Meg, the chief protagonist of *Wrinkle*, as Madeleine affectionately calls this book which won her the Newbery Medal in 1963, is good in math and science but not so good in English and geography. With this piece of information, L'Engle not only affirms for her readers that females can be good in math and science, but she also exposes the lie that they can't.

It is difficult to express how life-changing an event these awarenesses were for me. I believe that only the providential coincidence of my academic study of feminist ethics and theology with my rediscovery of Madeleine L'Engle's fiction could have produced this response. Discovering Madeleine's "gentle feminism" did not change my own feminist philosophy, which was not the sharp, hard brand. It rather confirmed my own belief that there was a better way to express its truths. More than that, what happened for me was the discovery of a scholarly project with a heart! My focus shifted very quickly from the academic writing of the Dalys and the Ruethers to the wonderful "this is how it should be" narratives of Madeleine L'Engle. But not before I wrote to Madeleine.

Here is something of what I wrote to this amazing woman:

> Coinciding with this return to L'Engle for me, is a one-month sabbatical from my teaching responsibilities at Elon College to work on feminist theology and ethics. At the same time I dove eagerly back into your wonderful books, I have been reading some more or less academic material relating to my official sabbatical assignment. I have been overwhelmed by what I have discovered, and this brings me to the purpose for which I am writing to you.
>
> I have become exquisitely aware of the fact that your books are woven out of all the themes, ideas, and dreams which make up the best parts of what is in theological, psychological, and sociological fields (to name only a few), being identified as an emerging feminist reality, awareness, energy! This awareness would probably not have zapped in on me so concretely had I not been reading your books at the same time I was reading about the character of the universally emerging feminist consciousness.
>
> Now, to the point. I would very much like to do a study of all of your theological and ethical standpoints in general, and from the feminist perspective in particular.

In my letter, I asked Madeleine if as far as she knew, anything like this had been done with her writing and ideas. I also provided her with a long postscript that gave a bit more focus to what I was talking about:

> I can't resist saying one more thing. The themes which are such an integral part of your writing: oneness with nature, brotherhood/sisterhood, peace and justice, community, cooperation, etc. are the very emphases which the emerging feminist consciousness embodies. I very much believe that in the emergence of a new holistic human consciousness (the best and brightest of the male consciousness and the female consciousness) lies the cultural shift which will help all of

> humanity come to grips with the environmental crisis, hunger and poverty crisis, and nuclear crisis. I have great hope! I am convinced that you do too!

My letter was dated January 11. Madeleine's reply was dated January 26. This is a portion of her answer:

> As far as I know, there has not been any study done in the area that you mention and it sounds fascinating to me. I am sending your letter on to my agent, Robert Lescher, 115 E. 71st Street, New York, N.Y. 10021, as I like to keep him au courant of all such ideas. I am sure he will be interested.
>
> I was very lucky in being brought up as an only child in a completely non-sexist family, where it never occurred to me that there was any reason that I could not do anything I wanted to do.

Of course, I began to read everything Madeleine had written and proceeded to fall in love with all of her wonderful books: fiction, nonfiction, poetry, and autobiography. It was the beginning of a wonderful journey! My additional research never disappointed me. In her stories, with their characters, themes, plots, and story lines, Madeleine L'Engle affirmed for me the acceptability of a new way of knowing, of perceiving reality, a way that may be considered the intuitive way, or perhaps better yet, the way that allows the marriage of intellect and intuition. She had been doing this in her stories for over forty years.

It is my belief that Madeleine L'Engle has "listened" her way into the reality of human wholeness. Through her stories she has raised, and is continuing to raise, the consciousnesses of her millions of readers with integrity and grace. I suggest to you that in her obedience to her muse, which I strongly suspect is a combination of the Holy Spirit and the universal unconscious, Madeleine has intuitively discovered and ingeniously brought before the human family for their consideration a new way of knowing universal reality. I think particularly of the message of human equality young readers are exposed to in her gentle and redemptive stories.

My journey with Madeleine's books and ideas led me into a wonderful relationship with her and her ideas and beliefs. This included, among other things, developing and teaching a course at Elon College called "The Religious Dimensions of the writings of Madeleine L'Engle," visits to her homes in New York and Connecticut, participation in several of her writers' workshops, and the opportunity to do extensive research, with her permission, on her papers which are collected at the Buswell Memorial Library in Wheaton, Illinois.

I wrote a grant and was able to bring Madeleine to Elon twice: once in 1989 and another time in 1996. Both times, she stayed at my home in the town of Elon. The second time she came, she preached the Baccalaureate sermon and received an honorary Doctor of Humane Letters Degree. This was in 1996. I wrote the citation for her for that event.

As I read Madeleine's writing, the idea for my book *Suncatcher* was born. It is regrettably now out of print. The first edition was published in 1995; Madeleine's dear friend, Luci Shaw, wrote the foreword. The second edition, published in 1998, was different in several ways. First, the title was changed from *Madeleine L'Engle, Suncatcher: Spiritual Vision of a Storyteller,* to *Suncatcher: A Study of Madeleine L'Engle and Her Writing.* In addition to Luci's foreword, Madeleine wrote one. Another addition was a copy of the complete text of Madeleine's Newbery Medal acceptance speech.

After the publication of *Suncatcher* I had the opportunity to be the compiler of two books of L'Engle's writings. The first was *Glimpses of Grace: Daily Thoughts and Reflections,* published in 1996. This was a book of inspirational readings. To prepare for it, I reread everything Madeleine had written to that date, marked the passages that I believed were inspirational, assigned them relevant titles, and put them in order for 366 days in a year. The second book I compiled was called *Madeleine L'Engle Herself: Reflections on a Writing Life,* published in 2001.

This memoir bears witness to the life-changing power of my January "Aha!" experience, which marked the beginning of my friendship with Madeleine L'Engle and the birth of *Suncatcher.* For both of these "gifts" and so much more, I remain extremely thankful twenty-five years later.

Oh Madeleine

by Carole F. Chase

Oh Madeleine,
Silent now the voice—
Still the pen.
We shall never know
What kind of grandmother
Meg Murry would have been.
What happened to Charles Wallace,
Whom Vicky Austin wed, or
Whether Zachary Gray was finally redeemed.

Quiet now, the storyteller we have loved and listened to
And been enchanted by for half a century,
No Christmas poems this year, or ever again;
No more regular Epistles to report on how your days have been.

Our sorrow and grief are mixed
With the benediction of good memories—
Your wonder-filled stories
Are peopled with families, adventures, love, and joy,
They reflect your solid confidence in God
Spilled out on every page,
These are your gifts to us ... your legacy,
These will simply have to be enough!

Yes, this is truly a never-ending story.
In the lives of scores of lovely characters,
In over fifty books;
In memories and friendships shared
Your great faith lives on,
With us and in us.
Thank you!

Sept. 6, 2007

Madeleine in a publicity photo, 1970s.

Kindred Spirit, Sister, Friend

by Phyllis White

Phyllis White took workshops with Madeleine L'Engle on the West Coast and was her friend for nearly twenty years. She has written poetry, interviews, and reflective articles for church publications.

She came into my life when I was nearly fifty, already a grandmother. My friend had given me a copy of a new book she thought I would like, *A Circle of Quiet* by Madeleine L'Engle. I did not know the author, but I was immediately drawn to the title. However, the book sat on my desk for a while, as life swirled busily around me, with little time to sit and read. I often glanced at it, and planned to one day find my own "circle of quiet" and read what this writer had to say.

When at last I went alone to the sea for a few days I took her book with me and began to read. The more I read, the more amazed I was to discover within those pages a woman I already knew—a kindred spirit, a sister, a friend. This was someone whose life, though outwardly very different, had followed inner paths so similar to mine—whose feelings of awkwardness, of being different, and of being an outsider, and whose thoughts and questions and doubts and faith journey were parallel in many ways to mine. She was someone who, though we had never met, *knew* me—and I knew her. It was an exciting discovery. If only our paths had crossed, I fantasized, we would have recognized each other, and become good friends—as young girls, wives, mothers, and now, grandmothers. But my life had always been on the West Coast, and hers on the East, and this was not going to change. Only a miracle could make it happen.

With the passing of years, I continued reading her work—*Wrinkle in Time,* of course, journals, poetry, novels—and became even better acquainted with this remarkable woman. Then one day, another friend came along and told me that the renowned Madeleine L'Engle, my fantasy friend, was coming to California! She was going to teach a workshop at Mt. Calvary, a monastery just two hours from my home. My friend urged me to go.

The thought terrified me. Though I had been writing for many years, I had never aspired to be a professional writer, or to be "published" (except for a couple of self-published collections, and several church publications). If I went to this workshop, there would be writing assignments, and perhaps we would even be asked to read our work aloud—a very scary thought. But when, to satisfy my friend, I nervously called to inquire about it, I learned that only twenty-eight people could come, and the roster was already full. I would be number sixty-nine on the waiting list. I was relieved. I gave the secretary my name and phone number, but I was certain I would not be called. Then, five months later, the phone rang. I was invited to attend the workshop.

I remembered reading about Madeleine's strong belief in "God's synchronicity." I knew I had to go. With my heart pounding in my throat, planning to hunch down somewhere in a corner and just listen, I climbed on the Greyhound bus and went to Mt. Calvary.

The old monastery sat high on a craggy mountain at the end of a narrow, winding road, overlooking the beautiful city of Santa Barbara and a wide expanse of unbroken sky and glistening sea beyond. The air was clear and fresh, filled with the fragrance of native sage, oak trees, and wildflowers, and inside, a subtle blend of scents: lemony furniture polish, incense, fresh bread baking. The monks were warm and welcoming. The other folks were all strangers to me, but I shall never forget my first glimpse of Madeleine.

She moved slowly, gracefully, down the gleaming wood floor of the long, high-ceilinged hall on the way to the meeting room. She seemed almost majestic—so tall, with her stylishly cropped hair, robed in a glorious aqua and purple gown, and, I was surprised to see, sturdy barefoot sandals. That, I was to learn, was the essence of Madeleine: part awe-inspiring, with her head in the heavens, and part earthy, with her feet firmly planted on the ground.

We were at the monastery for five days, a writing workshop followed by a silent retreat. The first evening we sat in a large circle in the richly appointed meeting room, and introduced ourselves. Then, after talking a little while about writing, she assigned us to write a story. My mouth went dry and I wanted to hide. I didn't know how to write stories! I tried, for much longer than the hour she instructed us to work that night, but only managed a fairly good beginning. Of course, we each had to read our story aloud the next day. Some were excellent. And Madeleine didn't critique, as I had expected—she enthusiastically affirmed what she liked about each, and sometimes gently made a suggestion or two. She complimented my beginning. She made us all feel like writers. Suddenly I was no longer afraid. At last I was physically present with the friend I had met in her journals. She was real.

We didn't talk with each other much that first time, not because she was unfriendly, but because some of the others had met her before, and were eager to talk with her, and I was still nervous and shy. But when she returned to Mt.

Calvary the next year, we had several good conversations and began to become acquainted. (And I finished the story I had begun the previous year.) The Impossible was happening. Madeleine and I were becoming real-life friends.

Several times she invited my husband Jerry and me to stay with her when we were in New York. The first time, when we walked to the front door of her apartment building and were met by her doorman, George, he gave us an envelope with her key in it, and our names on it in her handwriting. We felt like Important People! We rode the rumbling old elevator up to the ninth floor and opened the door into the legendary apartment that I had read so much about. Madeleine was not at home, but her snow-white cat, Tatiana, greeted us with a friendly meow. As I looked around, I had a mixture of feelings—of familiarity, being at home, being in a dream. Somehow, the walls filled with paintings and portraits, family photos from several generations, floor-to-ceiling bookshelves, and worn and tasteful furnishings, including her grand piano—all seemed just the way I might have pictured her home. I felt honored to be there.

Phyllis White and Madeleine.

Madeleine immediately embraced us with her warm hospitality. She and I had become friends, but until that day Jerry had not met her. He was usually at ease with new people, but having heard so much about her, he was still a bit uneasy, being in the home of this renowned, accomplished, celebrated woman. He had never been good at correctly pronouncing people's names, and the first day he accidentally called her "Marilyn." She immediately reacted. "It's *not Marilyn,* it's *Madeleine!"* Then, for emphasis, she added with a twinkle, "*How*-ard!" We all laughed, and from that time on, now and then, they would teasingly call each other "Marilyn" and "Howard."

Then came the year when I was facing surgery for what was very likely to be a diagnosis of cancer, and was scheduled to return to Mt. Calvary for another workshop and retreat with Madeleine. My doctor recommended that I not cancel my plans, but go there first, "where people will pray," she said, "and then come back and have the surgery."

On the first night, as I sat in the chair on Madeleine's right in the large circle in the now-familiar meeting room, I hoped that she would begin the introductions to her left, so that my turn would be last, giving me time to collect my thoughts. Instead, Madeleine turned to me and said, "Let's start with Phyllis—where are you this evening?"

I took a deep breath and blurted out my concerns about my upcoming surgery. I apologized in advance that I might not be able to focus well on the assignments, but wanted to be there anyway. And Madeleine said, "Let's stop right now and pray for Phyllis and her doctors." So a roomful of strangers, and Madeleine, my friend, prayed. And during that workshop I wrote some of the best stories I had ever written—and even finished my first sonnet.

When the retreat was over, Madeleine was leaving for an engagement in Hawaii, but wanted to stay in touch and know what my diagnosis would be. I promised to call her when she returned home to New York and let her know what was happening, but she couldn't wait. She called from Hawaii every day until she returned home, and then every day after that, when I went through my surgery and recovery. And contrary to my medical prognosis, Madeleine assured me, in her strong, authoritative voice, "You are *not* going to die! Sometimes I know these things. I knew that Hugh was going to die. And I know that you are *not* going to die." I had no choice but to believe her. And as soon as I was able to travel, she insisted that we come to the Cottage for a while—"because it's a healing place," she said. And indeed it was.

I was learning more and more about the generous love of Madeleine's huge heart.

During the ensuing years, our friendship deepened. We stayed in each other's homes and became acquainted with each other's families and tended each other during convalescences from illness—mine from bouts with cancer; hers from hip

Jerry White and Madeleine.

surgery and other complications. We held each other during times of crisis, loss, and grief. When she stayed in our home one year, Jerry played his guitar and sang some of the old hymns, spirituals, and folk songs for her, many of which she had not heard before. Later, when she was no longer traveling, and we were at the Cottage for several weeks to visit and help care for her, she borrowed a guitar for him to play, and every afternoon she asked him to sing. She always requested that he finish with the song that had become her favorite, and she sat listening with a wistful, faraway look in her eyes as he sang, "I am a pilgrim and a stranger/just traveling through this wearisome land."

And when Jerry was diagnosed with terminal lung cancer some time later, she phoned often, and when he died, she grieved with me—on the phone, and again, at the Cottage, the "healing place," walking in the spring meadow, watching glorious sunsets, and listening to tapes of him singing.

Madeleine and I traveled together and attended workshops and retreats that she led up and down the West Coast. She loved to share her friends with each other. At Vancouver School of Theology one year, she instructed me to find her good friend Sher. She said we needed to get to know each other. So I obediently hunted for Sher in the upstairs hallway of the dorm where we were staying. When I found her, we sat on her bed and talked for hours, and though Sher is young enough to be my daughter, we have been good friends ever since.

Sher and I have many wonderful memories of times together with our friend Madeleine. One year, hip surgery prevented Madeleine from traveling west as she had planned, so Sher and I went to her. We helped care for her at the Cottage, while Barbara, her loving caregiver, took a much-needed vacation. We remember long drives in the lush green countryside, having lunch at Madeleine's favorite spot, Aspen Gardens, where she always ordered spanikopita; wading with her on the slippery stones in Dog Pond; picnicking atop the hilltop she could see from her bedroom window; and, one eventful night, driving around and around a lake in pitch-dark, pouring-down rain, looking for a favorite French restaurant in the woods that she *knew* was down that road—and sure enough, eventually, it was. At night, she had to wear a huge black and purple brace up her entire leg and thigh, which she christened "Darth Vader," and it took all three of us, often amidst boisterous laughter, to get that leg hoisted into bed each night.

Madeleine was always looking for fun. Once, when she was exhausted from a long day of speaking and book-signing at Fuller Seminary in Southern California, she realized that there was a Jacuzzi at the hotel where she and I were staying, and she wanted to try it out. Not having a bathing suit didn't faze her. I got out an oversize T-shirt with a huge Mickey Mouse on the front that I had brought for sleeping, and she put it on, tossed a towel over her arm, and unselfconsciously strode to the pool, where she was happily refreshed.

Her loyalty was fierce. One year, when I had finished six months of chemotherapy, and had no hair, I was wearing what I hoped was a somewhat stylish beret to cover my baldness. When we arrived at Mt. Calvary, a young monk, newly in charge of hospitality, told us that there had been a mix-up and there was no room for me. Perhaps they could put me up at the convent down the hill? Madeleine was incensed. Drawing herself to her full height, she snatched off my beret and loudly charged, "Do you see this woman? She has just had chemotherapy! You will *not* send her away! And if you do, I will go with her!" "All right, all right, don't worry—we will figure something out," said the chastened monk. I put my beret back on my bare head, and he quickly managed to find rooms for both of us.

That was the year that Comet Hale-Bopp was visible from the mountaintop as it passed over the western sky. One day Brother Lawrence, Mt. Calvary's resident photographer, excitedly told us that he hoped to get some good pictures of it that night. Madeleine, of course, was thrilled, and could hardly wait until dark. We all stood on the porch outside the massive front doors of the monastery, Madeleine with "her head in the heavens . . . and her feet firmly planted on the ground," catching her breath with wonder as the comet streaked across the blackness of the star-filled sky. Copies of the pictures that Brother Lawrence took still bring back the awe of those shared moments.

During the later years, when she could no longer travel, we spent time together in Goshen. We went on long drives. We sometimes had lunch at Aspen Gardens, or dinner at Applebee's. I enjoyed cooking in the spacious and well-equipped kitchen in the Cottage. We spent many hours around the dining table, as candles burned low, savoring food and conversation and music, often with family members or good friends. She affirmed and encouraged my writing. We laughed a lot. We prayed for each other and for each other's families. At night, after the activities of the day, it was just the two of us, lying on her bed, reading Compline, and talking, talking, talking far into the night. As the years went by, we continued to discover more and more parts of our journeys that we had in common—life experiences, insights, wounds and heartbreaks, joys and enlightenments. She was ten years older than I, and very wise, so I learned much from her. I loved her—and was privileged to be a recipient of her unique and all-embracing love.

Her friendship was an unexpected gift that came at a late and special time in both of our lives. Now she is gone, and I miss her sorely—but my heart is full of memories, and I give thanks.

Every once in a while, miracles do happen, don't they?

A Personal Tribute to Madeleine L'Engle

by Kay Buckley

Kay Buckley, a close friend of Madeleine's, gave the following tribute at a memorial service for Madeleine at All Angels' Church in New York City on September 9, 2007. Kay, who took many of Madeleine's writing workshops and assisted in teaching others, has published her poetry in magazines. She wrote the second part of this essay in June 2009.

My husband Jimmy and I met Madeleine in 1989 through our son, Rob Buckley. Rob died fourteen years ago at the age of twenty-seven. He was Director of Community Ministries here at All Angels' and there is a Memorial Gallery here at the church in his memory. For a long time he had been telling us that we had to come to this church he had started attending with some of his friends. One morning when we visited, we walked in and Rob pointed to the front of the church and said, "Do you see that lady sitting up there? That's Madeleine L'Engle! She goes to this church, she wrote *A Wrinkle in Time*, and she is my friend." Our introduction that day began the Buckley family's eighteen-year friendship with Madeleine.

Madeleine was a great friend and mentor, wise, and fierce in her faith. We spent hours discussing all manner of things, especially spiritual matters. She told me that way down deep in my heart I would always be a Baptist girl. This she said, as my sponsor, after I was confirmed in the Episcopal Church! She had a keen sense of humor. She often suggested that we get two cans and string a wire across the Hudson River so we could cut down on our phone bills between New York and New Jersey.

Madeleine held writers' workshops in her apartment in New York for eight years just for the congregation of All Angels'. She offered workshops all over the world, but All Angels' people held a very special place in her heart. She touched countless lives in so many ways. She was available, approachable, and unblemished by fame. She adored people, and people adored her in return.

After my son's death there was a time when I could not pray. "Don't worry about praying," she said. "We will pray for you!" It was as simple as that and pray they did.

In the church service, we sometimes prayed in small groups. One Sunday I told her I was not moving my chair into the "circle of prayer." I announced I wasn't praying, I wasn't talking to God. She locked her eyes with mine and in that famous voice said, "Move your chair into this circle. You do not have to pray. All you need to do is "be.'" So, I obediently joined the circle and I just "be-d."

A few weeks ago a friend and I drove to Connecticut to visit Madeleine. An incredible gift and miracle was waiting for us. She was awake and sitting up in bed. For four hours she was totally in the present. We remembered, we prayed, we laughed and cried, we had Compline and Eucharist, and even sang songs. That was her last great day here on earth. Shortly after that she began her journey Home.

This week I received a note from a friend that said: "I have been told that you visited Madeleine regularly and were able to get her out over these past months. This is truly a treasure and gift for the both of you. Because of the communion of saints, I feel that your physical visiting with this dear one has in some ways represented us all and our love for her. We are all sending love to the family and seeing visions of angels welcoming her into the unending celestial dinner parties of the beyond. I can't wait to see her again there. And with that, the tears come flooding with bittersweet loss and joy."

When my father died many years ago, a friend sent a telegram that said. "Our loss, heaven's gain." Certainly those words ring true when we speak of our dear Madeleine. Our earth is poorer, but heaven is so much richer. Thanks be to God.

More Memories of Madeleine

I was sixteen years younger than Madeleine. She often reminded me that she could have been my mother, a very young mother, but my mother nonetheless. I sensed that she liked that idea. I think it pleased her to think of me as a daughter. In reality we were more like "girlfriends."

One indication of a good friend is the ability to be in each other's company and not have to speak. Madeleine and I instinctively knew what the other one was thinking. Sometimes, after a rare period of silence, we would smile and then start to laugh, because we usually knew the thought that neither of us had bothered to say out loud.

There are many memories of times we shared together and with our families. The kaleidoscope of those experiences encompassed the full spectrum of life in all its complexities. There were tears of laughter and joy, and a fair share of tears of sorrow. One of the deepest bonds that Madeleine and I shared was the loss of

Madeleine and Hugh, China, spring 1986.

our sons. She had been an incredible fortress for our family after our son Rob died. Years later, after her son, Bion, died, she would look at me with stormy eyes that simply said, "You know how I feel." And I did.

We discovered that we had similar experiences in our younger days. We were both energized by words, writing, and reading; we both played the piano. Neither of us was attracted to mathematics. However, Madeleine did do a considerable amount of dabbling in quantum physics. The one big difference was that, as she often stated, she was a cradle Episcopalian. I, on the other hand, grew up in a large Baptist church. Quite a difference, and yet in many ways surprisingly the same.

Madeleine was my sponsor when I was confirmed in the Episcopal Church. As I stood in front of the congregation that evening, I glanced over and saw her sitting in the front row. She kept pointing to her face but I had difficulty deciphering what she was trying to tell me. Then I saw the tears coursing down her cheeks. She wanted me to see that she was crying. She did not cry often. I cried all the time. That night we cried together.

During the summer months, Madeleine and I would talk for hours each night on the phone. We would dream dreams, ask questions and strive to answer them, ponder love, especially God's love, grace and mercy, redemption and forgiveness. We talked of life in general and not so general. We always finished with Compline from the Book of Common Prayer. The ending was always the same. I would ask her to say The Lord's Prayer in French and then in Latin. It was music to both my ears and my soul.

What wonderful times our families shared when we were with her at her beloved Crosswicks Cottage in Goshen, Connecticut. There were days we would sit on the big screened porch for hours, have lunch, feel the soft breezes, gaze over at Mohawk Mountain rising majestically in the distance, and listen to the low

Cornelia Duryée Moore, Luci Shaw, Madeleine and Kay Buckley, 1998.

melodies of the wind chimes in the trees. I can hear them still.

On beautiful clear days, some even in winter, we would sit on the back deck and "read the clouds." We discovered shapes of all kinds and made up stories about the people and animals that we saw in the azure sky. We never wrote those stories down. We should have.

Periodically we would take long rides on the winding country roads. Sometimes our son David would drive, and Madeleine would sit beside him as the co-pilot. Once we ended up on the top of a mountain where it seemed as if no car had ever gone before. Invariably we got lost on the way home. I can still hear Madeleine saying, "No, turn right here, or is it left?"

Spending New Year's Eve with Madeleine at the Cottage grew into a treasured tradition for my husband, Jimmy, and me. The three of us would enjoy the last hours of the old year and then ring in the new, tucked away inside the house on those freezing January nights. My, it was cold! But the twinkling lights of the large Christmas tree in the living room always radiated a warmth and liveliness that no cold could obscure.

I remember a particular New Year's Day when we started preparing dinner before returning to New York City. Mealtimes were always celebratory for Madeleine. She loved to cook and to entertain. That day asparagus was on the menu; asparagus with Hollandaise sauce! Jimmy was on the far side of the Cottage when Madeleine and I wrestled in the kitchen with the ingredients for the sauce. Somehow the stick of butter slipped out of her hands and in our attempt to catch it before it slid across the floor, we knocked the top off of the blender with the cream still churning inside. By the time we stopped laughing, we were both saturated with butter and cream. It was literally dripping from our eyelashes. What a sight, what a mess, what fun! We cleaned up, started over, and dinner was, eventually, a huge success.

It always was!

(Top) Crosswicks, (bottom) the garden shed at Crosswicks.

Supper with Madeleine

by Stephanie Cowell

Stephanie Cowell took workshops with Madeleine L'Engle beginning in 1989. After a career as an opera singer, she formed a singing ensemble and a chamber opera company and produced concerts and Elizabethan festivals. She is the author of Nicholas Cooke: Actor, Soldier, Physician, Priest; The Physician of London *(American Book Award, 1996);* The Players: A Novel of the Young Shakespeare; *and* Marrying Mozart, *which has been translated into seven languages and optioned for a movie.* Claude and Camille, *a love story about Claude Monet and his model/muse Camille, will be published in the spring of 2010. Her essay is adapted from an article published in* The Living Church *in 1999.*

The things in her apartment overlooking the Hudson River in New York City became old and familiar to me over the several years of our friendship, and I looked for them whenever I went to see her. The heavy silver water pitcher, decorated with silver flowers, which was her mother's and which we always filled with ice and the coolest, purest water. The Russian eggs on the side table in the dining room, the platter precariously placed atop a cupboard (my husband, rushing by, once sent it crashing to the floor). The portraits on the wall, family pictures in the hall, old posters of her late husband's theatrical career in the kitchen, and in the guest bathroom a framed advertisement with a young, pretty, dark-haired Madeleine L'Engle, marking the publication of a book. Everywhere were thousands of books, shelves lining the hall. Some of the dining room silver had been hidden in the dirt while Southern ancestors fled the approaching Union armies a long time before. I have forgotten the details.

She, on the other hand, remembered nearly everything. The names of a thousand or more friends and writers who depended on her and loved her, anecdotes of history, the day on which a certain psalm fell in the monthly office readings, the living and the dead. What she did not recall precisely sent us to her Bible concordance and other books. I saw in her a spirit of eclecticism, a mind shockingly young and curious in a body in her seventies and then early eighties. Her five-foot

924 West End Avenue.

ten-inch frame possessed twice my energy, endurance, and creative stamina.

Each of the many relationships in our lives is a journey, and we meet each other at different passages on the way. Ours began when I first saw her across a chapel in an Episcopal convent in the Upper West Side of New York, sitting quietly, hands on her lap, waiting to begin her writing class. I was a student, in my middle forties and desperately trying to find a publisher for my first novel. She had been through the pain of such publication rejection well over twenty years before, which ended when *A Wrinkle in Time* was taken by Farrar, Straus and Giroux. I was her daughter Josephine's age and raising sons in their late teens; her house was filled with granddaughters hardly older. I was to begin a new marriage in the next few years; her long and much adored one had recently ended in her husband's death.

Intimacy, as she always said, takes time. Though she said many true and wise things, there was none more so than this. Yet how any person could keep in her heart so many thousands of her fellows is still beyond me. One day I found her in bed, somewhat tired; she had been a little ill, but still managed to dictate some

Madeleine, Stephanie Cowell, and Sally Lowe Whitehead, around 1998.

seventy letters that day. Each year her writing students, mostly New Yorkers and a few others, gathered for a potluck dinner in her house and filled the rooms. In this extraordinarily full life, she had somehow found a place for me.

But I do not want to write an ordinary thing about her (if such a thing is possible), or to recount the chronicles of the rich life which she has portrayed in her books. Rather, I want to share something of the small, personal story of our friendship since the night I walked into that convent writing class and, after the first session, blurted, "Will you read my novel?" and, at her consent, floated the two miles home without feet touching the ground.

My novel was about a sixteenth-century actor who is a friend of Shakespeare and who becomes an Anglican priest, subjects that interested her. When W.W. Norton gave me a contract, her huge bouquet of flowers arrived the next day at my door. After that, she read all my books in manuscript. Her belief in my work was everything to me.

Once I called her with some now-forgotten author's angst, and then slunk away when I understood I had taken her from her own writing. From her class came my writing group, which met for ten years. Yet God worked in even more mysterious ways through our friendship, for I would never have known the man who became my husband but for her. An admirer of her work, Russell had corresponded with her for many years. He then introduced her writing to a close friend, whom I subsequently met at one of Madeleine's retreats and who introduced me to Russell. Madeleine had us to her house for a sumptuous meal and guessed before we did that we would make a life together. Some year and a half later she stood up with her cane at our wedding (her knees had long been troublesome) and gave me away.

Sometimes I called her Mama Madeleine. At a wiltingly hot wedding reception we both attended, I called her my Melting Mentor. I shall never forget her extraordinary generosity once in the time before I met my husband. She lay in her hospital bed, hardly days after both knees had been replaced, and summoned me to her, having heard rumors of a disaster in my life. As I sat there gasping out the story, she lay quietly listening. Later she invited me to sleep some nights in her apartment. Between her mending knees and my wretched, weeping heart, we comforted each other, though most comfort came from her... there was someone to take care of and she did it.

Her writing was but one facet of the woman's generosity. In those days, as I recall, her granddaughters, who had lived with her for many years, were moving out. Someone else would come soon. She drew people. Her hands and heart were open to give; though sometimes disillusioned (she could be dismissive and scathing when appalled or hurt), she believed in the goodness man can achieve and the total mercy of God.

What could you give to someone so beloved? I like to think that we who were her New York writers (and we ranged from journal writers to those, like myself, who had published a great deal), were fortunate by our proximity to form a kind of family around her. She saw us in love, in our marriages, at the birth or adoption of children, in the success or failure of our writing projects. She also lived through our heartaches, perhaps a dubious result of caring. As if her hours extended indefinitely, she seemed always somehow to have enough for those who needed her. She traveled a great deal, and we were always glad when she returned to the city.

"Come to supper!" she would say buoyantly a few times a year, and when I rang the apartment bell, I would hear her bellow, "Coming!" as she made her way on long legs under some exquisite, embroidered skirt down the hall of books. My husband and I had arrived with food to cook, but more often she had cooked herself, which she loved to do (and she was a superb cook), as long as we would manage the dishes. Once I sat near her bed with our friend, the late novelist Isabelle Holland, and ordered Chinese food. Then her other friend, Barbara Braver, came in and we had a startling, sudden conversation about families and parents and longing.

Generally, though, we dined at the gracious, heavy table in the room overlooking the river, with pure cool water in the silver pitcher and candlelight shimmering on goblets and Russian eggs and homemade food. There was the blessing and then the company. Sometimes at the end of the evening we would read the old Anglican service of Compline, which closes the day, together. I would borrow some books of hers and leave her one I knew she would like.

Walking to my own home afterwards in the darkness down West End Avenue, I sometimes thought of the mystery of how people come into each other's lives and grow into a kind of family. Hers ranged over the world. It enriched me and I am glad to have been part of it.

Darling Madeleine—until we meet again!

A Decade of Transformation and Grace

by Katherine Kirkpatrick

Katherine Kirkpatrick, the editor of this collection, took Madeleine L'Engle's CHS workshops beginning in 1989 for several years and elsewhere for nearly ten years. She writes primarily for young adults and occasionally publishes reflective essays. She is the author of seven books, including The Snow Baby: The Arctic Childhood of Robert E. Peary's Daring Daughter, *and a forthcoming archaeology book about Kennewick Man. She is an associate lay member of the Community of the Holy Spirit.*

We arrived, most of us strangers to each other, highly expectant and eager to answer our individual calls to adventure. It was the fall of 1989. We had climbed the flight of stone steps at 113th Street on New York City's Upper West Side to a bright red door. The portal led to the Community of the Holy Spirit, an Episcopal convent, where an extraordinary author named Madeleine L'Engle was teaching writing workshops. We came together not unlike the characters in Madeleine's beloved novel, *A Wrinkle in Time*, about children who join forces with angelic presences for a fantastical journey.

One participant who entered the brilliant scarlet door said she'd heard of the workshop when a flyer was blown by wind smack onto her face in a rainstorm. Stephanie Cowell, a friend who was an opera singer and now a novelist, learned of the workshop while cooking meals at a church soup kitchen. As for me, a twenty-five-year-old editorial assistant at Macmillan Publishing Company, I'd heard of the seminar from a red-haired copy editor who was Madeleine's godchild. She had gone to the same private school as Madeleine's own children, now also grown. The school was affiliated with the convent, and one of the ways Madeleine helped support the convent was to teach writing there and donate the income to the sisters.

Three of us young editorial assistants had our minds set on taking the Tuesday evening class, which was to unfold over the next five weeks. Miraculously, it seemed, exactly three spots were still open. But there was a problem. Still looking for an apartment in Manhattan, I was commuting two and a half hours from my parents' home on Long Island. When I phoned the convent later, I mentioned my unwieldy subway and train rides; everyone knew how dangerous they were late at night. "We have extra rooms," the sister on the other end of the line replied cheerfully. "You can stay here!"

It was as simple as that. On the night of the first class, I rang the bell and the same nun I'd talked to on the phone, Sister Jerolyn Mary, greeted me at the door. Some of my nervousness dissolved as the plump, middle-aged sister, her black habit mantling a round, pleasant face, beamed me a smile. She showed me to my simple "cell," provided with a clean single bed and a strip of carpet. A short time later, one of my three Macmillan friends, Mike, a young editorial assistant who also had a long commute, showed up, and Sister Jerolyn Mary led him along the convent's silent hallways toward another small, modest room.

Many of the details of that night elude me now. After ten years of workshops with Madeleine there, and in two other monastic settings, my friends' faces and what we said and felt together have become a jumble. But I remember well my first impression of Madeleine. In a back row of the chapel, bathed by the sisters' sweet singing of psalms at Vespers, I caught sight of her tall and dignified form, bent over in prayer.

Afterward, going to dinner in the convent basement, I was bold enough to place myself directly across from her at the long table. All around us the writing students took their seats. I'd soon regard them as kindred artists, and in time, some would become friends for life.

The nuns served themselves last from the buffet, and many of them, who were shy around the visitors, ate in an adjoining room. Sister Sarah, a petite, elderly sister with a curved back and crooked smile, always joined us. She was passionately interested in science and enjoyed taking part in conversations. It was she who cooked our meals. Years later, I found out that Sister Sarah's bountiful feasts, which included such treats as nuts and avocados in the salad, prevented the sisters from breaking even when they hosted our workshops, which had been intended as fund-raisers. So in subsequent years, the meals became a little more spartan, much to Sister Sarah's chagrin. I sensed it was the highlight of her week to spend all day baking homemade pies for us.

Our workshop followed dinner with the sisters and came before Compline, the last of a day's five religious services. This sequence of activities, unlike any writing workshop I'd ever heard of, encouraged bonding and helped to establish a non-competitive tone among the participants. During the hour-long class, we'd read aloud to the group Madeleine's assignments, like this one: "Write about a favorite female character from the Old Testament; write for an hour; try not to think; try to get out of your own way."

I wish I could recall more of what Madeleine said to those twenty participants around the big oblong table in the third-floor conference room. However, I can envision her clearly: tall and stately, commanding and regal, wisps of short gray hair falling close to her head, wearing a loose-fitting, floor-length dress of rich purples and blues (the colors I always associated with her) and a large necklace of silver pieces that fit together like a sun and crescent moon. In the way she spoke, she emanated kindness, greatness, and strength; such a rare combination, it seems, could only come from love, and spiritual power. My hopes of what the author of many favorite childhood books would be like lived up to those high ideals and even more. To know her was indeed to step fully into *A Wrinkle in Time*'s magical realm.

Other recollections of that first evening come to mind. After Compline service, ending with the chime of a bell and a nun extinguishing candles on either side of a gold crucifix, Madeleine left the convent for her apartment in the neighborhood, and a final noisy confusion of writers saying their good-byes filled the hallways and subsided. The large, three-story building suddenly and mysteriously emptied out. All but one or two of the nuns slipped away to the cells in their private enclosure somewhere in that vast-seeming building of many rooms. Then there came a complete and profound silence.

My friend Mike and I started toward our tiny cells. A young, attractive nun named Sister Heléna Marie emerged from somewhere, found us both, and asked if we wanted to walk the convent's dogs. They had a large, mostly black dog, Joshua, a mixture of Rottweiler and Gordon Setter, and another mutt half his size, Jenny, who was brown with droopy Beagle ears. So in a few minutes there we were, dogs pulling on their leashes, walking along the narrow, tree-lined park of Riverside Drive, in the cold and damp air of late autumn, with a light rain falling.

Even New York City has its periods and secret hamlets of utter quiet. When people and cars and taxis depart, there is sometimes a hush. That night was one of those times, with its cool mist in the air, illuminated in circles around the street lamps. It was all part of the enchantment of meeting Madeleine and spending an evening with her and the sisters. I remember asking myself, "Where am I? What just happened?" Had I spent days in the convent, or just hours? It was hard to know. A sense of newness and excitement filled me.

In the years to come, I'd still feel that quality of wonder around Madeleine.

Those who, like me, took part over and over in Madeleine's workshops and retreats, were each seeking (even if unconsciously) a particular experience of the heart that comes through spiritual community. We stayed on because we were finding it. At the vortex of a boundless, holy energy field of light, Madeleine drew souls looking—within the same artistic and spiritual context—for inspiration for their work and growth, healing for their inner and outer lives, and transformation for their whole being. Like attracts like; and a vibrant community with dozens of people at its core, and over a hundred in its wider circles, came into being in the Manhattan area through Madeleine. The image of lighting one candle with another and the name Madeleine gave to her Connecticut house—"Crosswicks"—appropriately convey how those who knew her carried light from one to another, equally, and also to other people who would accept and trust it.

Madeleine often talked and wrote about the natural harmony of events, and was interested in such themes as God's time and our time; she reminded us that spiritual knowledge will be given, can *only* be given, at the right time. Thinking back over my years of knowing her, I'm aware and deeply grateful that I entered Madeleine's circle at exactly the right moment. In that decade, beginning in the fall of 1989, Madeleine was seventy-one, recently widowed, and being well established in her writing career was devoting herself largely to teaching. In my case, I was recently out of school, in my mid-twenties, single, and had little in the way of responsibility or commitment. How fortunate I was, at this juncture and age, to love her and be loved by her, to be influenced by her, and, with many years ahead of me, to practice living in spirit and knowledge and begin passing on something of it to others.

Then, like a "tesser," a "wrinkle in time," the shining chasm of Light and the opportunity of knowing Madeleine closed, just as it had opened, in perfect symmetry. In 1999, I married and moved to Seattle and, the following year, gave birth to twins. Within a year of my relocating to the West Coast, Madeleine, who'd moved from being unsteady on her feet to a walker, then to a wheelchair, gave up public appearances. The last time I saw her in person was in 2000; and soon after that, with mounting health concerns of all kinds, she moved into a nursing home in Connecticut. She died in 2007.

Life has given me the fortune to know a great many special people; many of them I met through Madeleine. What was it that made Madeleine the most radiant, the most extraordinary of them all? I've never quite been able to answer this question fully, but I can begin to understand by considering Madeleine's blend of rare qualities. She not only viewed life with a great sense of wonder; she lived with an absolute, unshakable belief in Divine Purpose. She emanated power, knowing, and love. Her capacity for love was enormous. She immersed

Sanna Stanley, Madeleine, and Katherine Kirkpatrick, 2000.

us in the wellspring of eternal Spirit. She acquainted us with the mysteries of the cosmos, of the beauty and dazzling nature of the planets, stars, and galaxies, and of angels. At the same time, she was altogether human and vulnerable. I saw her angry at times, even childishly cranky; whatever it was she was going through, we all knew it, and I don't think she could have concealed her feelings even if she'd wanted to.

My friends and I came to Madeleine with a wide variety of joys, concerns, and questions, and at times arrived at her workshop table, or doorstep, in varying degrees of spiritual brokenness and confusion, psychological distress, grief, even in a state of collapse. There was no matter too great for Madeleine's undivided, serious attention. Nor was any matter too small. Every concern was a spiritual concern—as was every solution. One class at the convent began with a writer entering the room weeping. On the way there, she'd seen a Canadian goose hit on the Saw Mill Parkway. Madeleine responded at once with her absolute conviction: "Now let us all join hands and pray for the goose. And I *know* the goose will be all right."

I think many of us, especially the young writers, came to her aspiring to write a good book and have it published. This hope Madeleine always met with complete certainty; we could all succeed. Writing was mostly a matter of discipline to get to one's desk, and the rest of it was "getting out of the way"—to the other side of reason, to incarnation—joining in service and in creation with God. After that, if we truly wanted it, if we called on the courage to keep at it, the writer's life was ours. It was unpredictable and accompanied by angst and pain, but all the same, it was glorious. (Then, as if we hadn't heard the story many times, she would repeat the exhaustive search she'd undergone to find a publisher for *A Wrinkle In Time.*)

Madeleine was like a grandmother to me. She was also like a minister, a trusted advisor. As a mentor in writing, she never actually critiqued what we wrote and she rarely gave pointers about technique. She was, more accurately, a Wise Woman and guide, maybe more than a little like the angelic presences in

A Wrinkle in Time, Mrs Who, Mrs Whatsit, and Mrs Which, who had ways of bringing out the best in their earthly students by magnifying the students' inherently good qualities.

Our workshops were about writing, yes. But as we all realized early or later, Madeleine approached writing mostly as an entry to the larger Cosmos—and its core. We came to Madeleine because we wanted to be loved. And we wanted peace in our hearts. We wanted to know we were on the right track—not just as writers, but on our life journeys. We wanted to be less afraid and more courageous. We wanted to have lives out of the ordinary. We wanted to understand the Universe, our roles in it, and know God. We wanted to know that for our own sakes, and for our loved ones, that death is not the end. We wanted her to remind us that there is in God's Universe nothing random or pointless, ever; all is part of a grand design. Most of all, we wanted someone of her stature, someone with authority, to tell us: *our lives matter.* This is what she affirmed to us, over and again, and what I never tired of hearing: "God made you and me and all of Creation. God is concerned with every galaxy, every atom and subatomic particle. Everything that happens to each and all of us is of cosmic and eternal importance."

Madeleine gave weekend retreats in the Community of the Holy Spirit's Melrose Convent in Brewster, New York. Those taking part spent a day and a half, usually, in silence. All of us felt nourished in one another's company, without conversation, reading on the comfortable couches in the living room of the convent's guest farmhouse (if we were quiet enough, a mouse might scurry across the threadbare Oriental rug). We shared meals, drank tea, wrote in journals, and walked along the winding country road under the lofty covering of immense sugar maple trees.

Madeleine introduced each retreat in the same way, with the same metaphors: "Ease into the silence. If you see sharks, you'll know to back off; and you'll know you will be all right, and enter more fully into the silence, when you see dolphins." And she always gave us this wise advice: "Check your problems at the door, along with your shoes. You can pick up those problems again when you leave. You may find that they have become smaller, or no longer exist." This easy-going, grandmotherly approach to spiritual discipline served as my entry into a meditation practice that has been part of my life now for nearly twenty years.

I look back at those ten years of workshops and retreats with enduring pleasure, and sadness and yearning, too, because two of my closest writer friends and many of the sisters are no longer with us—and Madeleine now is gone. It wasn't that Madeleine's circle and I lived that decade easily and without care; our lives were far from easy. Being near the center of a great energy vortex meant transformation; and while we grew with joy, art, creativity, community, and friendship, we progressed through healing and the challenges of releasing pain. During the quiet periods of a retreat, those with particular needs met one-on-one with Madeleine for conversations and prayer behind closed doors. Because I often knew the others in the retreat well, I was at times aware that horrendous problems were being prayed about—such as the death of a child or a painful divorce.

Most of the healing naturally took place outside the retreats, with the guidance of professional counselors. But since so many of us took the workshops and retreats multiple times, and met independently in smaller writing groups, the spiritual community that formed through Madeleine created an integrated system that infused and supported all we did. Madeleine and the sisters gave a safe environment for people, mostly women, to know each other in our truest and best selves, and to form the most trusting and understanding relationships possible. I cannot imagine my life without the friends I met through Madeleine.

In my own case, for my particular trauma, which I experienced early in my Madeleine decade, the spiritual community served as a wide and healing, golden net that was by miracle in place, ready to receive me, when I took a great fall. (And afterward I found the net could change shape. I could pull this transparent gossamer sack around me for protection. I carry it still.)

The event took place when I was twenty-six years old. Through Jane Gardner, one of the closest friends I met through Madeleine, I came to live northeast of Manhattan on City Island. We shared with several others an old house, a former telegraph station surrounded by boats and, on both ends of the island, lighthouses. It was a charmed place; I felt exquisite freedom there. I came to know quite a few colorful personalities, among them an ornery retired captain of oil tankers. And I entered a passionate romance with a thirty-two-year-old rigger of sailboats, Johnny McCauley. It was brief. He died on a freezing day in January 1991 when a motorboat he was in overturned in Long Island Sound.

I was wild with grief and shock. On top of that, I felt judged and questioned at every turn, even by well-meaning family. ("What was he doing on such a tippy boat, a floating junkyard, out in the middle of winter? Why didn't he finish school and set out to find a real job? Considering you didn't know him very long, you seem to be taking this awfully hard.") Few people knew what to say.

Johnny's drowning happened about ten days before the annual potluck dinner Madeleine gave for workshop members past and present. It was held in February that year in her magnificent apartment at 924 West End Avenue in Manhattan. Madeleine was having mild stomach problems, so she stayed in her bedroom while she let the reunion go on without her. (Another hostess would have surely canceled, but it was typical of Madeleine's generosity—some might add, eccentricity—to allow a crowd of fifty or more writers to take over her kitchen and living room.)

Tatiana.

She arranged for one visitor at a time to come in to see her. At my time, I entered her bedroom. Madeleine, wearing a nightgown with lace at the collar, was sitting up in a large four-poster canopy bed with lacy pillows and, by her side, her pure-white cat, Tatiana.

I think all I could do was start to pour out the tragedy. Madeleine said, "I know..." I remember the depth of compassion in her eyes. "They told me. I've been waiting for you." I hugged her and cried. There were no questions, no judgments. There was no telling me I shouldn't cry or confront my pain head-on as I was doing, or love someone I should not have loved. Nor did she tell me, then or ever, to look for security in life that does not exist. Or that life should be in any way easier, or the world less painful and dangerous than it is. She gave me, instead, the great gift of acknowledging my pain. And without her using words, I felt her powerful affirmation: Johnny McCauley's life mattered, greatly. It mattered on the great scale of the Cosmos. My life mattered. She loved me. God loved me. Then Madeleine said aloud, with a surety and conviction that was hers alone: "You'll be all right."

In the months that followed, Madeleine encouraged me to write about Johnny and what took place on the Sound. I wrote letters to him, which I read to the writing group that had formed a year earlier (and would be a significant part of my life for many years to come). Madeleine said to me, "As you write, you will depart more and more from the facts that happened, as you come closer to knowing the truth."

Madeleine, in that still raw day of winter, and in the distance toward healing I crossed afterward, was the one who knew what to say. She had spoken, with her arms around me, "You'll be all right." And I was.

Several years after the tragedy, in the fall of 1995, I published my first book, a novel titled *Keeping the Good Light*, set on City Island in a bygone era when it was renowned as a shipbuilding center. The central character's brother drowns in a boating accident. Unlike the real-life personality, this character didn't die in an odd job for forty dollars cash. The man commanded an important position as rigger for an America's Cup yacht. But most important, he was regarded highly, loved by all; his life, too, mattered.

One person at a time, Madeleine made a worldwide impact. And what did we give to her? She adored people, and I know she enjoyed our gatherings, our candle-lit dinners, singing with us the Tallis Canon as our prayer before the meal. She found reward in teaching and lecturing; she must have, or she wouldn't have done so much of it. Why? Did she see us transform and become a little wiser, reach higher perception, in her presence? Did she see the smiles on the faces of people who had been in deep mourning or distress? Observe sharp personalities softening? Did she notice small gestures of kindness from those who had usually been too self-involved to consider others? Did she see timid people taking courageous steps? These changes in us would have moved her; and I think very little was veiled to her sight.

I believe she was pleased by all the books her workshop writers eventually published. Certainly, the independent writing groups that came together outside her classes gave her happiness and pride. Her response to the new friendships and marriages born in her groups was great joy.

I hope, and in the end trust, that Madeleine knew the profound honor and the heart-filled awareness of God's grace whenever someone revealed that she had touched a life. Is she now, in another realm, like Mrs Who, Mrs Which, or Mrs Whatsit, looking down at the Earth, seeing all our souls growing bright in patterns of illumination with the galaxies and stars? Are the concerts of lights, our lights and those of many others, joining and dispelling the darkness? I hope so. In fact, I'm sure that is the case.

Madeleine's seventieth birthday at the Cathedral Diocesan House, November 1988.

A Sonnet for Madeleine

by Elsa Okon Rael

Elsa Okon Rael is a playwright/lyricist whose works have been widely produced. She is also the author of four children's books. After Elsa took Madeleine's 1989 workshop at CHS, she hosted a writing group that met at her home. In subsequent years, Elsa's apartment became a meeting place for the entire community of New York writers in Madeleine's circle.

A Sonnet for Madeleine

A soul whose very presence was healing
What hadn't she known of sorrow and pain?
We were restored by her warmth and feeling
Yet always she spoke her truth loud and plain

Her laughter was bright as sun overhead
Her voice spoke in words that never misled
Her touch was a haven to the forlorn
Her fingers, a balm, though weathered and worn

We read her our writings with hopeful mind
Yes, hopeful she'd hear our work as true art
Always her comments were cogent and kind
Her understanding came straight from her heart

Her gift was to give, again and again
For such was the essence of Madeleine

On Setting a Space

by Sanna Stanley

Sanna Stanley is a writer-illustrator and a fine artist who works in many mediums, including etchings and watercolors. She is a popular workshop facilitator in art and creative writing in schools on the East Coast. She both wrote and illustrated The Rains are Coming, Monkey Sunday, *and* Monkey For Sale, *an ASPCA Henry Bergh Honor Book for Fiction and a Notable Trade Book for Young People. She also illustrated* Amistad: The Story of a Slave Ship *by Patricia C. McKissack. Sanna attended Madeleine's CHS workshops in 1990 and 1991.*

I was in my own cold attic bedroom of a New England farmhouse when I first met Meg Murray—another oldest—on her dark and stormy night. The distance between her world and mine seemed no thicker than the unfinished plywood walls that kept the wind and scratching pine branches outside. Like Meg, I was an awkward adolescent whose family did things very, very differently than the neighbors in our small Vermont town. Like Meg, I was always tripping over pieces of myself. When I met Meg, I felt understood.

I tripped my way out of that small Vermont high school and into one college and then another, hoping that I would land in the right vocation. My missionary kid background gave me the sense that in order for my life to be meaningful I ought to be a teacher, nurse, social worker—in essence, someone who serves others. But I wanted to be an artist. An artist and a writer.

Because the culture I came from was evangelical Christian, I sought the will of that all-knowing and magnificent God on this matter of what to do with my desire, not quite sure I was supposed to have such a desire. There was also the problem that I never quite heard the voice of God as clearly as those around me claimed to. I tumbled through college, and settled for a minor in art. Then I took a risk and applied for a graduate program in painting. I loved painting, loved exploring the colors, textures, slide and slap of paint on canvasses and the spackle patterns on the floor of the studio.

But painting didn't pay my bills, and I wondered about writing and illustrating children's books. I was in Bible Belt country, and was advised to make Christian art and write Christian words, so I attended a conference of religious publishers in Wheaton, Illinois. Although this hooked me on publishing, I was not at all convinced that religious publishing was the place for me. It wasn't my next vocation I left the conference with, but something else. While in Wheaton, I meandered into the bookstore where a book whispered echoes of my own feelings about the whole matter of religion and art, Christianity and writing. The title was *Walking on Water: Reflections on Faith and Art.* The author was Madeleine L'Engle, none other than the author of that Meg I'd met back in high school.

Here was an author who echoed my questions and offered me possibilities outside of the Christian world, yet was also a person of profound faith. Madeleine allowed herself (and me) doubts, Madeleine (and I) asked hard questions and didn't settle for easy answers. "Serve the work," Madeleine wrote, and gave herself (and I took) permission to be both Christian and Artist, but not necessarily in a hyphenated sense.

It was undoubtedly that permission that vaulted me, eager and shy, to The School of Visual Arts in New York City. I took Madeleine, my favorite author and in some ways a spirit type familiar, with me. Her books were stacked together with my journals and sketchbooks, lest I should lose vision and need to remember. I didn't even think she'd mind, not terribly, one Sunday morning when my ragged copy of *Walking on Water* turned into a sketchbook. I was reading on the stoop of an Upper East Side church when I couldn't keep from drawing a pigeon that watched me watch him. In a way, I was writing into Madeleine's world as she'd written her way into mine.

My MFA curriculum combined writing and art, words and pictures in varied and experimental ways. As part of the program, we were to select a professional in the field to "mentor" us. In retrospect, I see that the assumption was that this mentor would be a professional illustrator, one who would not only inform our artwork, but serve as a professional contact. I wasn't so savvy. Madeleine L'Engle lived in New York, didn't she? I strummed my heartsong.

When Books of Wonder advertised a reading and signing by Madeleine L'Engle that spring, I wrote the date down in my sketchbook. Waited. Then, because an extra ride downtown wasn't in my student budget, walked from East 74th St., where I lived, to West 18th. I took my place in a very long line of people possessively cradling books to be signed.

Self-conscious, I hesitantly and resolutely approached this great—and large—presence of a woman. Seeing what Madeleine looked like was somewhat of a shock (she struck me as ostrich-like) and I was nervous. But because I'd known some "other soul" part of her so long, I just told her the truth, that I had no book for her to sign, but I'd wanted to meet her for ever so long. She plucked a Books of Wonder postcard from a pile, asked my name, and signed, "For Sanna, Ananda! Madeleine L'Engle." Then, with a grand flourish of hand, she bestowed that blessing on me.

With people pressing at my back, and Madeleine's assistant pulling from the front, I forced out my query, inarticulate, and too fast. "I'm at an art school—get to choose a professional in the field—do you ever mentor?"

No, she didn't mentor, her assistant told me, but call the Community of the Holy Spirit on 113th St. and inquire about Madeleine's workshops. I wrote this down in my sketchbook. Called as soon as I got home, and had to suffer the time it took for my message to be returned, then felt the rubbery texture of disappointment. The next workshop was full.

Would I like to be on a waiting list?

Yes.

There is some genius to fate, and, at the very last minute, I received a call saying that a spot had come available.

I went.

Madeleine, Katherine Kirkpatrick, and Sanna Stanley, around 1995.

And discovered that Madeleine's words on writing were less important to me than her presence. I'd already moved away from the need to be literal in the translation of my faith. Yes, I was in a writing workshop. Madeleine gave homework. She led exercises. Around a crowded table in a cramped conference room, we shared characters, wrote into Bible stories, re-membered our lives by recalling, remembering, and putting flesh back on dry bones. There was incredible wisdom in our writing tasks. Think. Jot down notes if you need to. Then write. Half an hour, forty-five minutes, or one hour, a set time frame was important, but more important was the permission to just do it, get it down. And once that was expressed with vehemence, Madeleine voiced an imperative: Do Not Edit. I believe that command was the caress that summoned the muse for those of us who hoped—desperately—to have a muse within.

We listened, hushed with a sense of awe, to each other and our own voices, voices that read aloud and writing voices that sang unique harmonies from each of us. It was a shy surprise that we were each brilliant with Madeleine presiding.

"Listen to the story," she said. And because Madeleine was listening to us, we resonated with her particular form of magic, the power of listening. We listened to each other, listened to her, and learned to listen to our writing.

It takes an extraordinary human being, one actively and consciously *being* human, to invite a disjointed group of people into a room and turn that room into a space where magic happens and mystery hovers. Yes, we lit what I called "Holy Spirit" candles and we met in a convent, and we prayed at the table, but it was something about Madeleine in her greatness, about Madeleine letting go and trusting the process of writing, the work of listening, that invited each of us to also be bigger than we knew we could be.

I call that gift "setting a space," a mystical ability to create a little world that others can inhabit. I call Madeleine's regal sitting at the head of the table "holding a space," a sensation that would continue for the duration of the evening. It was what my tai chi teacher speaks of as holding a string of pearls without breaking the connection. It is what a grandmother does when she holds a baby until the baby falls deeply asleep. It stems from understanding that the gift of one's attention is the greatest—and most powerful—gift each of us has to give.

We wrote under the spell of the promise that Madeleine cared.

And because she cared, we did, too. Cared enough about our own writing to join writing groups, some of us brazen and confident, others timid and terrified. All of us saying, "I want to write." And be published. We reminded ourselves that Madeleine L'Engle had said it was important for your (our) work to be seen, to be heard.

And we cared enough for each other to become friends, encouraging and nurturing not only our writing lives, but our worldly ones, too. We've attended weddings, anniversaries, joyful book signings, and sadly, funerals.

Our circle of friends that began with Madeleine's workshops at the Community of the Holy Spirit expanded like an accordion does when it swells with music. We gathered, added, lost, and stayed in touch.

Even though we meet infrequently now that we have moved on with our lives, and in many cases moved out of the New York area, when we do get together I am at home. In spite of differences of opinion, style, and tastes, I feel understood, like I did when I met Meg as a teen. We have appropriated Madeleine's gifts as our tools, which is as it should be.

We listen intently; whether to a writing or a life story, we try to listen without judgment. We strive to give permission always, permission to just do it, get it out, go ahead and write it down, and then "Don't apologize, don't explain," permission and an imperative learned from Madeleine, "Just Read."

Even though we banter, argue, and cajole, and no matter where we meet, we are in a sacred space, like an overtone still reverberating from the spell that Madeleine set for us so many years ago in that cozy convent room.

Sanna Stanley and Madeleine, 2000.

Orbits

by Judith Lindbergh

Judith Lindbergh took Madeleine L'Engle's CHS writing workshop in 1990. Her first novel, The Thrall's Tale, *about three women in the first Viking Age settlements in Greenland, was a Book Sense Pick and a Borders Books Original Voices selection. Her work has appeared in* Archaeology Magazine *and in connection with the Smithsonian's exhibition "Vikings: The North Atlantic Saga."*

We circled around the long oak table in the narrow upstairs conference room of the Upper West Side convent—St. Hilda's House on West 113th Street. I hadn't even known until that night that a convent existed amidst the townhouses and pre-war apartment buildings I passed every day on my travels around New York City.

Nineteen years ago, on that crisp autumn evening, I was a naïve, twenty-something Jewish girl from New England living in New York and working on a novel that had a lot to do with spirit. It was a topic I'd been grappling with for as many years as I could recall and through which I sought to escape the narrow shelter of my upbringing. I was fascinated with spirit and belief, with understanding their myriad manifestations across cultures and time.

I recalled the poignant magic of first reading *A Wrinkle in Time* and its subsequent installments, not fully recognizing in my eleven-year-old mind that underlying that magnificent story and those wonderful characters was a Christian faith of which I knew very little. At a friend's suggestion, I had joined this writing workshop to be close to the woman who had written those words.

Perhaps I thought I could reflect some of Madeleine's brilliance, absorb some of her energy, tap into some of her connection to spirit that made her seem otherworldly to me. Perhaps I felt that, by passing close to Madeleine L'Engle's light, I might somehow gain some clarity and understanding of the many questions—both literary and spiritual—that continually spun around in my work and mind.

But as I rang the bell at the convent door, I found myself tripping over the threshold of preconceptions: old prejudices about scowling, disciplinary nuns, the confining rigidity of convents, even Christianity itself with its strange rituals of smoke and incense and a figure on a cross that I found gruesome at best. All these things were utterly baffling to me—my preconceptions probably based more on middling children's literature than any personal experience. Still I sensed that, if I'd told my parents—which I hadn't—where I was going that night, they'd have tilted their heads and raised their eyebrows in pitying dismay. "Why? What do you think you're going to learn there?"

The sight of the young, bright-eyed nun smiling gently at me was the last thing I expected. "Welcome," she said. "Set your coat down here. You can go downstairs. The rest of Madeleine's students are having supper."

Supper? I didn't recall anything in the class notice about supper.

I wandered down the staircase, knowing I didn't belong. Apparently no one else noticed. I was guided into the golden light of the cozy kitchen, where other students encircled two pine tables laden with large platters of brown rice, steamed vegetables, nuts, and dried cranberries. The nuns' habits fluttered as they served and chitchatted comfortably.

I took a place at the end of a long wooden bench amidst this bevy of strangers. They all seemed to know one another, seemed familiar with this Christian world. Everyone already knew the prayers they murmured except me.

I ate timidly, perusing my company, certain each of these other writers was far more accomplished than I. But there was something else going on here beside creativity or ambition, something that had to do with kindness, generosity, and unadorned community, something I couldn't yet name.

When I realized that Madeleine was also sharing this modest supper, I nearly choked on my food.

After the meal, we ascended the narrow, slightly sloping staircase. I didn't know it at the time, but the creaking ascent was ushering me, not toward the grandiosity of my imagined literary success, but into a close-knit shelter where lives would intertwine and a net would be woven that would be my safety and support for many years to come.

We filed into the conference room and tucked into tight corners. By the time we all had settled in, we couldn't even open the door unless someone moved. The intimacy was unnerving, despite the hospitable surroundings. The room's walls were lined with heavily laden bookshelves. The air was appropriately musty. Steam through the heating pipes occasionally rose above an inconspicuous drone, adding rattling counterpoint to the rustle of papers and subdued, slightly nervous voices.

We took turns reading around that table. I don't remember what I wrote. I remember little of what Madeleine actually said, though recently rereading some of the passages in her collected work, *Madeleine L'Engle Herself,* I realized I'd gleaned many of those wise kernels around that table.

Madeleine sat at the far end, beaming down on all of us, radiant as the sun. I say "beaming *down*" because she was extraordinarily tall, even seated; and her simple presence felt as nurturing as solar warmth.

I do recall that each week we had an assignment and a time limit in which to write. We were to store the fleeting moments of inspiration, like shaking up a soda bottle and building pressure up, then let it splatter in a free-flow of hopeful, judgment-less creation.

No judgment. Most of all, that's what I remember. There was, of course, good writing and bad. There were oh-my-goodness-I-WISH-I-could-write-like-that moments. Each was taken in kind. Madeleine embraced all of us. Out of trembling vulnerability, self-consciousness, and confusion, our unique thoughts took shape and form. We composed with growing certainty that our voices would be accepted with words and gestures of appreciation, hope and encouragement, suggestions and patient listening—listening that was absolute, beyond courtesy to keen attention. In that listening was the gravity that rooted us and showed us that each of us mattered, no matter the content or the skill of our words. It was the invisible force that drew our thoughts, and the souls that breathed them forth, together.

Madeleine never knew me very well, nor did I really know her. I took her workshop only that once. I was never invited for dinner like some of the others; I wasn't one of her inner circle. I was a distant satellite, but once drawn in, I found the gentle pull of her community irresistible. It bound me not only to her, but to all those who were similarly drawn, part of the gravitational energy that circled at varying distances around her.

For ten years, six women, most of them Madeleine's former students, became my confidantes, my critics, my patient, incessant nurturers, my wet shoulders to cry on. And I became theirs. We met on monthly Saturdays at Elsa Rael's midtown apartment and shared the tradition of food—partly in remembrance of the convent table, but enhanced significantly by "Bubba" Elsa's bountiful kitchen. "Bubba" means "grandmother" in Yiddish, and Elsa was another of Madeleine's rare Jewish students. Instead of the Christian prayers we'd said at the convent, we shared the Hebrew prayers I knew, but always before Elsa said *hamotzi,* we all joined hands and each would pray aloud for ourselves and for each other.

Every winter, many of Madeleine's students would reassemble in her West Side apartment, descending like a meteor shower bearing dishes of home-cooked pierogies or grain salads from the corner gourmet market, pale reminders of the simple pleasures cooked by the convent nuns. We crowded into Madeleine's L-shaped kitchen, rummaging through cabinets for platters and serving spoons, helping slice the bread or heat up another of Elsa's wonderful stews.

Peggy Harrington and Judith Lindbergh prepare one of the grand buffets at 924 West End Avenue, mid 1990s.

We sat at Madeleine's feet. I remember that, after the food had been enjoyed amidst an endless flow of "How are you's" and "You look terrific's," we each took a turn to tell our tale: what had happened or not happened in the year we'd been apart, and what we hoped for in the next. Some of us were deeply committed to our writing. Others had used it as an exploration of self, just one of several stops on the way to other fulfillments. Some told of marriages, divorces, births, the loss of a father or a son. Some had published, or not published, or wished to publish. Many—almost everyone—asked for prayers.

Our gathering was no longer about writing. Perhaps it had never been. It was about community and spirit, and Madeleine was our mentor and our guide. From her impetus, many other groups had formed, smaller constellations that mirrored the original but had taken on their own configurations, personal, vibrant, self-sustaining, independently alive.

For the last three years, I have nurtured one of those fragile constellations. Every Thursday night I enter through the broad oak doors in the grand façade of a 100-year-old high school building in my town. I walk along its umber hallways, listening to my boots clack on the tile floor, then drop down into the bowels to an overheated room where two plastic folding tables are pushed together.

There's no kitchen of cooking nuns, but some of my students have taken to bringing bags of Hershey kisses, pretzels, or brownies, and sharing a bottle or two of wine poured into paper cups. It's inelegant, but perfect, in this new circle of busy working professionals and exhausted parents, where sneaking away for two hours each week is decadence itself.

When I begin each new session, I don't start with a prayer. I've kept spirit to myself in this secular setting. But I always begin by talking about my writers' group and the circle of hands that drew us together around a table laden with food.

It is a new orbit. And if I am its center, it is only because I was closest to the start of the first concentric circle, orbiting for a time, then flying off into the greater space of emptiness that begs to be filled with the eternal warmth of love and acceptance and luminous generosity. I'm a dim shadow of the sun that I once circled, but my students have grown brighter from the reflected light I've shared. I often speak of Madeleine, and offer excerpts of her wisdom along with guidance from other writers who've shed light on the dark and lonely universe of the writer's work. When Madeleine passed, we dedicated our autumn session to her memory.

After evenings at St. Hilda's House, the nuns always invited us to Vespers. At the time I didn't know that Vespers was the twilight prayer service, but I didn't need to. I took a seat in the tiny chapel at the top of the townhouse, and the nuns would sing. The music rose to the low ceiling, penetrated the roof, and soared upward. I drifted along with the subtle turning of candle-smoke and melody. Lit and dimly shining, it carried me to the heavens.

To that tendril of spirit, I have clung and am still clinging. I am orbiting with the rest of you, circle upon circle of those who learned from Madeleine herself or from her words. With each turning, we share in the spirit that embraced us, urging us a little farther on our journey.

Quickened Dust

by Pamela Leggett

Pamela Leggett, a close friend of Madeleine's, attended her workshops and retreats beginning around 1990. She began her career in creative therapies, which later led her into the world of writing. Currently Pam and her family are hosting a mission project in Pisco, Peru, the site of the massive 2007 earthquake.

Within This Strange and Quickened Dust

O God, within this strange and quickened dust
The beating heart controls the coursing blood
In discipline that holds in check the flood
But cannot stem corrosion and dark rust.
In flesh's solitude I count it blest
That only you, my Lord, can see my heart
With passion's darkness tearing it apart
With storms of self, and tempests of unrest.
But your love breaks through blackness, bursts with light;
We separate ourselves, but you rebind
In dayspring all our fragments; body, mind,
And spirit join, unite against the night.
Healed by your love, corruption and decay
Are turned, and whole, we greet the light of day.

—Madeleine L'Engle, first published in *Lines Scribbled on an Envelope* (Farrar, Straus and Giroux, 1969)

One evening in New York City, late in the 1970s, I arrived home to my apartment ready to relax. My roommate met me at the door with the words, "Madeleine L'Engle is downtown signing books. We have to go!" I protested, tired and unwilling to turn around and go back downtown. She insisted, saying, "You may never have this opportunity again. How often do you get a chance to meet Madeleine L'Engle!" I reluctantly agreed and we made our way downtown

Madeleine and Pamela Leggett, early-mid 1990s.

to buy a book and have it signed. I remember that she was lovely. She answered questions and happily discussed her young grandchildren. It was worth the trip.

Years later, in the 1980s, I had moved to the Upper West Side, Madeleine's neighborhood, and now had numerous opportunities to cross paths with her. One dark and stormy night I came home tired, happy to kick my wet shoes off and fall into an easy chair. The phone rang. A sister from the Community of the Holy Spirit said, "You are on the waiting list to be in Madeleine L'Engle's writing workshop. It started last week and the second session is tonight. If you come over right away, you can attend the rest of the sessions." I was tired; it was raining. I didn't want to go, but it seemed an opportunity not to miss. I dragged myself out and down to the convent. From that group meeting on, my life was forever changed.

Little did I know that stormy evening that Madeleine L'Engle would become my mentor and dear friend. Little did I know that she would open a world of writers and new voices for me, that I would attend her workshop every year for many years. I didn't know she would reach out to me in friendship and that I would be called to stand by her through some dark times. I didn't know that, as her health failed, I would meet with her weekly to take her to the Sunday vesper service at the Cathedral. I didn't know that, even after moving to Montclair, New Jersey, I would get myself up and out to drive into New York on many a dark Sunday evening to take her in her wheelchair into the Cathedral to hear the evensong. How I now treasure those times together, the workshops, the services, the dinners we shared before I took her back to her apartment, the discussions, the laughter, the stories.

For Madeleine story was everything. She encouraged her writers to skip down that wild and wonderful road of cosmic questions, questions that couldn't be answered but could be explored in story with all its truth. Her style was supportive, elegant and quirky. The Bible, with its characters and situations, was her textbook. She shared herself with us and taught us to share with each other. She told us that when we entered the world of writing we entered the world of mystery, and to get ourselves out of the way. The writers she most admired usually turned out to be committed Christians, probably, she commented, because it took a true grasp of the love of God for a writer to go into the darkest depth of the human heart. She said that when she got to heaven she planned to sit on the lap of George MacDonald and stroke his beard.

My place at that table in the convent, listening to the others read, lives in my memory as one of the safest and most interesting places I have ever been. I loved the other writers' works. I loved my own exercises done under Madeleine's tutelage. When she was eventually confined to a wheelchair and I was the person pushing it through some public place, person after person would approach her saying, "You changed my life!" Once I asked her what it was like to have people saying that to her all the time. She responded, "I work very hard not to hear it!"

Madeleine loved her "writers" and often became friends with them. She invited them to her home, to accompany her places, to celebrate with her, or to just share their stories with her. Everyone looked forward to the annual writers' reunion party at her apartment. She attended weddings and funerals. My husband and I were thrilled that she arranged her schedule to be with us when we had our new baby baptized. After her failing health required her to give up workshops and events, she would often ask about everyone. She wanted to know who had moved away, published a book, gotten married, become a parent.

Madeleine was a woman of faith, regular in her attendance at the Eucharist, in her prayers and her discipline in reading the Bible and the Book of Common Prayer. She especially loved Compline, the prayers for the end of the day. She lived knowing that her God, who would not answer all of her questions, would never abandon her. Soon after Madeleine gave her last writers' workshop at the convent, I was asked to run a workshop at my church. I agreed because I had attended so many of Madeleine's and knew how they worked. Then I realized I needed to ask permission from her. Her response was enthusiastic and warm. She explained that the workshop was not hers; it belonged to the Holy Spirit. She looked me straight in the eye and said that more people needed to step up and start running them. I run a workshop every year now. Madeleine was right. It belongs to the Spirit. Everyone loves it.

I miss Madeleine. I am happy for every moment I spent with her. Those moments were varied indeed and toward the end of her life, difficult. But now every time I see the sun lighting up a silver cloud I think of her. I remember her vision, her energy, her commitment to God. I remember saying Compline for her at her bedside shortly before she went into her final coma. I remember how she pointed out that Jesus' Resurrection turned a terrible Friday into a Good Friday. For Madeleine that Resurrection has come. I wonder if she is sitting on the lap of George MacDonald.

Pamela Leggett, and Madeleine holding Pam's daughter, Krista, Cathedral Library, April 1995.

Madeleine

by Shellen Lubin

Shellen Lubin is a writer, director, performer, and teacher of theater and music. She has written, directed, and appeared in numerous plays, musicals, and cabaret acts and writes a weekly think piece online called the Monday Morning Quote. *Shellen wrote to Madeleine for the first time when she was in college, starting a lifelong correspondence that also included one silent retreat and several writing workshops.*

Madeleine

Madeleine
Like Proust's cookie
One whiff, one wish, one while in her way
And the images flow, flood my mind,
Fill my page
    A nun's devotion
    A skeptic's scrutiny
    A Buddha's acceptance
    A baby's wonder in this sweet bitter Earth
    And our redemption, and our resurrection,
    And our rebirth

Madeleine
Like the Hanging Gardens
Ancient, abundant, overflowing
A living Wonder now lost
Inspiring, embracing
Tempest-tossed
    A yogi's wisdom
    A rabbi's humor
    A pianist's fingers
    A choir's voice
    A wild child's awe for this sweet bitter Earth

And our redemption, and our resurrection,
And our rebirth

She flew beyond
Tesseracting
Beyond what most of us can conceive
Beyond what most of us choose to believe
Immortal dreams, immortal words, and immortal soul mesh
In all too mortal flesh

Madeleine
Like Halley's Comet
Science and mystery flash across the sky
Able to be seen by any observant eye
Both commonplace and divine
Here and gone.
Yet still here.
Yet still gone.

Madeleine in the Cathedral Library, 1989.

Memories of Madeleine L'Engle

by Jane Mylum Gardner

Jane Mylum Gardner, an elementary school art teacher in Wilson, North Carolina, is the author of two children's books, Henry Moore: From Bones and Stones to Sketches and Sculptures *and* A Gift to America. *She took workshops with Madeleine at Holy Cross and the Community of the Holy Spirit beginning in 1990.*

A Wrinkle in Time was rejected by twenty-six editors before it was finally accepted for publication, and until tonight, I could not fathom how Madeleine found the courage to have her agent keep sending that manuscript out after receiving so many rejection letters. Why didn't she give up? Now I finally understand why. Madeleine knew what her job on this earth was about. She was the one chosen to write down the story, and she knew clearly that her job was to serve the work before, during, and after the words became ink on paper. She was responsible for making sure the message got into print. Madeleine's gifts were numerous: she listened so well, and she could tell such a good story. She always led you along on her search for the truth. And that was humbling and so full of life. That was Madeleine.

As I read *Bright Evening Star: Mystery of the Incarnation* for the first time in the winter of 2007, I could hear Madeleine's voice reading passages to me. It was comforting to be in her presence again, to share in the twists and turns of her life, in spite of the fact that she had already found her heavenly rest.

The inscription in the book, published in 1997, reads: "for Jane, with love from Tahiti and Sweet Georgia Brown. Madeleine L'Engle." Tahiti and Sweet Georgia Brown are two of the black Labrador retriever pups that were born in December 1999 to Megan, my yellow Lab, and Brownie, the dark brown shaggy dog who roamed the woods and walked the sandy shores of Orchard Beach with us at sunrise. When I talked to writers gathered at Madeleine's house about my search for good homes for the pups, I never dreamed the "someone" who would adopt from the large litter would be Madeleine. After looking at the photos I brought along, she smiled and said she'd take two. I was so relieved to know they were going to a good home. Madeleine's son, Bion, named them

Madeleine and Jane Gardner.

Sweet Georgia Brown and Tahiti.

The first time I met Madeleine was around 1981, when I attended an ongoing workshop with Jean Houston, a visionary spiritual teacher. These Body-Mind games, held right in the heart of an expanding NYU campus, were called Dromenon meetings. We danced, drummed, chanted, and experimented with thinking kinesthetically and with time distortion. That particular Wednesday evening, Madeleine L'Engle was the guest presenter. I remember chanting, "The nature of love is to create, the nature of hate is to destroy." I resonated with Madeleine deeply, and walked out of the building into the bitter cold night air knowing I'd encountered a kindred spirit. Something about Madeleine set my soul on fire, pointed me in the right direction.

Once on the damp Astor Place uptown subway platform, I tried not to stare. Both Madeleine and Jean stood, elegantly tall, only a few feet away from me. I closed my eyes and savored the picture: two of the most brilliant women of the twentieth century stood talking in the middle of a crowded subway station—unrecognized. The super-energized Jean Houston with her long, brown flowing hair was probably twenty years younger than the wise, grey-haired, grey-eyed Madeleine. (She much preferred the English spelling *grey* to the American gray.) I was bursting with excitement from the energy I felt from an evening spent with them.

The two, bundled in winter coats and chatting away, seemed so ordinary and extraordinary all in the same moment. While Jean's exercises normally put my head in the clouds, Madeleine's words had placed my feet solidly on the ground. I promised myself I'd find a way to study with Madeleine. The opportunity didn't come until some nine years later—at a juncture in my life when the timing seemingly couldn't have been worse.

I'd just been downsized out of a job I'd held for eight years, felt depressed, and was afraid of spending the money. In spite of my fears, I took a very deep breath and signed up for a silent retreat workshop scheduled for January 1990 at Holy Cross Monastery on New York's Hudson River, because the writers' retreat that had initially caught my attention was full. Second best would have to be good enough.

And so I drove alone nervously to Holy Cross Monastery, praying that I'd find some new direction. The ground was covered in snow as I stepped out of the car and the rut I'd been living in. During the silent retreat, in which talking was not allowed except at certain defined times, I often sat next to a young woman with straight blond hair. We both took notes as Madeleine talked. Being enveloped in silence in such a warm atmosphere, praying, having limited sharing, focusing on what Madeleine had to say would be a transforming experience, although at the time I had no idea.

At the end of the silent retreat, I offered the blond woman and several other New York City-bound women a ride home in my car, in spite of the fact that it was miles out of my way to go into the city. It was the first time we had a conversation about Madeleine and the retreat, and there was much to digest. My car was full of writers with dreams, intent on moving ahead.

The blond woman was Katherine Kirkpatrick, and by the time we'd reached the city, she'd invited me to her recently formed writers' group. Some of these writers seemed amazingly accomplished to me, and I was intimidated by their talents. After several meetings, I felt I was not in the right place and I dropped out. The important thing, however, was that I'd connected with a large community of writers who all knew each other through Madeleine. At that time there were three writing groups in New York City that had grown out of workshops taught by her. Three months later, I joined another writing group that seemed less overwhelming to me. Members of this group included the poet Patricia McMahon, writer/illustrator Sanna Stanley, and writers Andrea Simon and Pam Leggett. Others came and went from our group, but the core members were present from the get-go.

In celebration of Madeleine's November 29 birthday, her workshop participants spread the word and gathered at Madeleine's home. My first experience of this celebration was in November 1990. Glorious dishes of food brought by as many as seventy-five people—some from different states—gathered to reconnect after taking one workshop or another from Madeleine. We sang a prayer of Thanksgiving blessing, then ate and talked standing up, and then had a "go-around" sharing session as we sat on the living room floor around Madeleine.

I will never forget the excitement, the magical feeling of being in her apartment, the joy of being in her presence, a dog or cat always near her. A baby grand stood at the north end of the living room and the hallway walls were lined with books, a hallway that led to the east side of the apartment, the kitchen; at the south end was a large dining room table and then further south, the bedrooms. Our winter coats were piled high in one of the guest bedrooms.

I would return to Madeleine's apartment for other celebrations, and one evening, I remember closing the door to the bathroom, glancing down on the typical Upper West Side apartment black and white octagon-shaped tiled floors, and thinking, Oh, my gosh, this is not a dream. This is real, and I am so blessed, so happy to be here. On each visit to her home, I took a different mental snapshot picture of Madeleine's life. Her dark writing table overlooked West End Avenue. Her beautiful comforter-covered bed raised slightly off the floor on a platform awed me. Sometimes, there was a terrified white cat hiding under the bed in one of those rooms.

I considered it an honor to help clean up in the kitchen both before and after people ate. I liked being in the kitchen, where women—and some men, I might add—moved in and out freely in search of spoons, cling wrap, or serving dishes. I liked covering up platters or bowls that traveled back home with guests or were put in Madeleine's refrigerator "for later." The feeling of belonging was omnipresent. Madeleine remembered something about each of us. Her warmth filled the living room. Writing was the medium as our lives became intertwined.

For the sake of continuity throughout the year, members of the three New York City writers' groups met on various occasions, mainly at Elsa Rael's home, to continue sharing good writing and more good food. Sometimes momentous, life-changing events were celebrated, such as books being published or bridal and baby showers being held. More than once, drafts or chapters read in Elsa's living room later found their way into print.

Jane Gardner and Janet O'Connell.

In 1998, the resulting community of writers informally named themselves A Circle of Friends. Their tribute to Madeleine, a booklet written in honor of her eightieth birthday, was self-published and shared among those attending Madeleine's birthday celebration at the apartment.

I remember another evening as we gathered around that conference room table at a Community of the Holy Spirit workshop when Madeleine asked, "What makes a great story?" and then she quickly answered her own question, grinning. "Nobody knows!"

I wrote the following notes at that conference table sometime in the 1990s:

> When you write, don't think or you'll just block your imaginative writing. We are so channeled to think only with the top of our heads. Let the heart think in the dark—let all of yourself work together. All writing is autobiographical. All of our characters are aspects of ourselves. We have to allow ourselves to see those other parts of who we are. When you let your characters grow in their own way, then you don't limit them.
>
> Get the four W's on page one. Who, what—the person ... where this person is doing it, and when the person ... the "why" can come later.
>
> Read and write every day. Your best teachers are other writers.
>
> Write before you go to work. Write when you are fresh. Get a job that doesn't drain you. The chief purpose of education is to do what you're committed to.
>
> When you don't think, your intelligence doesn't go away.
>
> Don't think—that's the difference between fiction and non-fiction.
>
> When you write, you listen with your ears to the story, NOT with your head. Know who your characters are and know them well. Listen to your characters.
>
> I am constantly surprised by my characters.
>
> You have to FEEL free to fail. It doesn't matter if it doesn't work. We learn from the things we do wrong. Ants don't make mistakes. Ants do what they do ...
>
> Madeleine writes and puts her work in a desk drawer and then reads it a few weeks later. As an artist, you can't judge your own work.
>
> When Madeleine wrote *A Wrinkle in Time,* she was writing something very different. It was breaking patterns. When you write, you are called to serve this gift.
>
> Bach broke all the rules. You are called to do the things you can't

do. Just as people have adrenaline to save a life, we also have a spiritual adrenaline.

We as writers are serving a calling. You can't know if your work is going to have universality. It takes 300 years. If it's good art, it's religious, because it has abandoned itself to truth. Vincent van Gogh went on painting even though he didn't sell but one painting.

We become artists because we have to make sense out of this world. We are all klutzes and failures trying to become whole.

You need only to claim the events of your life to make yourself yours—Florida Scott-Maxwell at eighty.

Don't try to be spiritual. Just dump stuff into your journal. *Our work* knows more than we know. Try to serve the work. The work has its own life and pulls you along.

Question: How to write dialogue?

Answer: Listen, you have to do it every day. You won't know your character is real until he says something that surprises you. If a character is going to be real, you must not try to manipulate.

Let the whole thing out. Write the whole thing out and then rewrite. Intellect and intuition work together. Intuition usually writes the first draft. Intellect usually does the rewrite. Far too often, the intellect tries to stop the intuition. Write it all out and then cut. Madeleine usually cuts the book in half. DON'T EVER THROW ANYTHING AWAY. PRINT IT OUT. You have to find the gate to let the water out. When you get writer's block, it's your head that's talking to your intuition. You have to break the pattern. Listen to music, lie down on the floor, swim.

John Brown to Madeleine: "If I don't believe it, then it isn't true."

You find your grand plan by plunging in and usually the project you choose to do will be too big. Inspiration comes while you're writing, not before you sit down.

Read sixteenth- and seventeenth-century writers if you want to know good grammar. We are becoming a vocabulary-deprived society.

It's not our ability, but our AVAILABILITY.

She suggests reading sermons by Lancelot Andrewes and John Donne. She mentions *The Holy Fire* by Robert Payne, a scholarly but poetic book, and *The Oxford Book of Mystical Poetry.* She recommends M.F.K. Fisher's cookbook *How to Cook a Wolf.* Other books noted: *The Irrational Season, Lives of a Cell;* and the article "The Futility of

Global Thinking" in *Harper's* September 1989 issue.

Writing is a way of expressing love and when it's not, then it's demonic. I will say it again, The nature of love is to create; the nature of hate is to destroy.

Your worldview is there. If you are deep and questioning, that is going to show.

There's more change in this century than in any other. God is not tame. There are no safe boxes, writing will open you up. Safety is not part of the contract… You have to risk.

Write through one person's eyes. STICK TO ONE POINT OF VIEW. Writing in first person is hard, third person is easier and that's how Madeleine wrote.

Character development: You have to move into someone else's heart, bones, and skin. Going into a character that's from another country or another sex is difficult.

We are paradoxical. We are noble and yet, we portray a mixture. I don't want to forget any part of myself. Regarding her own journal, what you write down, you tend not to forget. I write in mine to get it out. If you feel something emotionally, you forget yourself. If you write it, you'll remember what it was like to be a young mother or a teenager, you'll remember family fights.

In a world without heroes, perhaps we can write our own. We are all called to uphold our standards, to say "yes," when the rest of the world is saying "no."

Decisions must be made in your heart. Clean up your own backyard first. RENDER, do not report. SHOW, do not tell.

When you write for children, the ideas are more challenging.

Madeleine does not accept advance money and she doesn't hand in anything like a first chapter, because she doesn't want some editor to help create the book. Her husband, Hugh, would cut the book so that only the essential was left.

Right before the book goes to print, it's very good to read it out loud.

The worst criticism of all is indifference.

Assignment: Write a story with an angel in it and something about healing. "Fear not . . ."

Only one who can see the invisible can do the impossible.

Postscript: Today is Saturday, November 29, 2008. I have procrastinated writing the end of this piece for nearly six months. But this morning, I visited Madeleine's official website just to confirm what I thought to be true. Today would have been Madeleine's 90th birthday. Somewhere in heaven, I know there is singing and dancing and celebrating going on. Madeleine is in the midst of this celebration with a smile on her face, surrounded by angels, and the message she gives me this morning is, "Fear not, for I am still with you, Jane!"

The fact is, Madeleine's love is still available to me, and the memory of her, vivid. Because of Madeleine, I am more open to acknowledging the multifaceted parts of my own spirit, and to allowing space for invisible possibilities and guidance. Madeleine is still pointing the way to a grander universe, one I can allow, and to a path that, with added courage, I'm more willing to take.

Madeleine in publicity photo, 1994.

A Single Drop

by Daria Rydzaj

Daria once worked as an underpaid chemist with a biology degree. During that career, she co-authored one technical article. After retiring from the chemical profession, she published one short story. She has also written numerous editorial essays in local New Jersey newspapers. In 1992, Daria attended Madeleine's fall CHS workshop.

> "A single drop can't even make a puddle, but together all our little drops and God's planning can make not only a mighty ocean but a mighty difference."
>
> —Madeleine L'Engle: *And It Was Good: Reflections on Beginnings*

Because she influenced so much of my life, writing about Madeleine is no simple task. Her writings, both fiction and her reflections, speak to the artist as well as the believer in me. But Madeleine isn't the only person who has helped me with my art; indeed, there are others whose commentary and inspiration have directly influenced the stories I've written. These "others" were my writers' group. Without Madeleine, I would never have *met* any of these writers, and my life would have been less blessed.

I was fortunate enough to attend one of Madeleine's workshops at the Community of the Holy Spirit in New York in the fall of 1992. Madeleine was a believer in community as a spiritual necessity, and she urged us to pray together and eat dinner with the sisters at CHS before the class began each week.

After the workshop ended, alumni created their own community through writers' groups. These groups met on a regular basis to read and comment on each other's work in a loving, caring, and non-threatening environment. The encouragement of peers helped to sustain the writers during their time apart. Most groups met in Manhattan or its boroughs.

Some people belonged to multiple groups. Others, like myself, had a harder time finding the right group or finding a group that wanted a new member. Being from the New Jersey suburbs, and being a new mother, added to my difficulties;

a breastfeeding mom could not be depended upon to attend evening meetings held one state over. Even though my situation put me on the outskirts, a satellite amongst planets, there were still joyous celebrations to attend on occasion.

Foremost was the yearly party at Madeleine's apartment. This covered dish affair attracted writers coming from many areas. Some had attended workshops in places outside New York, so I never knew whom or what to expect at these gatherings. There was always the joy of meeting those I hadn't seen for a while, and then there was the food.

The first two years I remember bringing homemade pierogi, and cooking them on Madeleine's fabulous restaurant-style stove in that odd, L-shaped kitchen that would quickly fill with writers and quirky conversation. The hodgepodge of dishes always managed to complement everyone's tastes, whether the food was home-cooked or takeout from a restaurant or deli. We prayed, then ate, talked, and ate some more. I recall a liverwurst and onion spread one year that was heavenly, and I don't eat liverwurst! The desserts were usually decadent and divine.

After dinner we would all settle into the living room. Madeleine would sit with us and talk, then after a while each person would be asked to share something about themselves and their writing over the past year. As the years passed, the gathering grew so large that we had to be brief.

It was inspirational, being around so many accomplished writers. As I was unaffiliated with a group, the loving warmth of peers kept me actively trying to write and looking for advice on my work. At one of Madeleine's parties, someone suggested holding meetings so that local groups and "singles" could get together on a more regular basis. I began attending these meetings, which were usually held on a Saturday or Sunday afternoon at Elsa and Sol Rael's New York apartment. We brought food and our latest writing, noshed, read, and listened.

Because this group was larger than a typical writers' support group, there were strict time limits. It was here that I first heard the phrase "Time Nazi." This was the name given to the person unfortunate enough to have to keep track of the time during readings. Speaking from my experience as a reader, hearing that call of "time" could be a blessing, but as a listener it could be an annoyance. Many times I wanted to hear more, but our time was limited.

We also met at book launching parties, signings, or readings at bookstores to show support and to bask in the warm glow of the group. There were weddings, christenings, showers, and other celebrations where writers opened their hearts. When Elsa held a memorial service for her beloved Sol, many writers spoke lovingly of the man who had played computer chess for hours in the bedroom while we writers monopolized their living room. Sol never complained when our gatherings lasted long past afternoon and into the early evening. We miss you, Sol!

Madeleine and Tino, St. Hilda's House, 1980s.

It was at one of those Saturday meetings that Katherine Kirkpatrick and Jane Gardner proposed that I join their new writers' group, meeting on City Island. Finally, a group of my own! Our meetings were held monthly on Sunday afternoons/evenings. Katherine read to us from several manuscripts that eventually became books. Our stories changed and improved, as we encouraged each other over dinner and dessert to rework and "tweak" copy.

The community we formed lasted several years, and went beyond our writing. We were there for each other. I received much encouragement and support through a very tough personal crisis involving my son. We swapped stories and recipes, and through joys and grief, we became closer as the years passed.

But life goes on. The founding members of our group moved to different coasts (Northwest and Southeast!). Eventually, the group disbanded because of distance. Still, I consider these women to be "family of the heart." Whenever I see a writer from any of the groups, it's as if the years fall away.

Although I may not see my dear friends often, the fundamentals Madeleine taught me about the importance of community and the people we choose to surround ourselves with are very much a part of the way I choose to live my life. A support group for moms with children who have learning differences became a new community for me. The membership of that group is fluid, and some very deep friendships have formed. Friends at church give shape to another community. My son, Chris, has had much difficulty with his peers, but has found community and friends with a bawdy troupe that shadow-casts "Rocky Horror" every month in Montclair, NJ—thanks to the "Home of Happiness" group! It just goes to show that community is where you find love and acceptance without having to change who you are.

To me, community is so necessary. It is truly the heart of what Madeleine believed and of what Christianity teaches. Christ's "New Commandment" was to love one another. Isn't that the essence of community?

Of course even Madeleine wrote about her own anger and irritability with people at times. Her first meeting with her dear friend Canon Tallis was not exactly blissful, if I recall correctly. She was not afraid to let her characters feel the same way; think of Meg Murry's disagreeable attitude and her anger in *A Wrinkle in Time.* Yet in Madeleine's vision, community promotes tolerance, love and understanding, which brings joy. It includes people rather than excluding them. And I know that I love and appreciate people I might never have known or met, people that I would have overlooked, because of Madeleine L'Engle and her sense of community.

In November 2007 I was fortunate enough to attend the memorial service to honor our dear Madeleine. There I met with many of my precious friends whom I had not been able to see in years. Renewing friendships made the sad occasion a joyful one, which would have made Madeleine very happy. I was taken aback at how many people remembered me, and how many names I recalled despite the years that had passed without an annual party at Madeleine's apartment.

All of us were present at Madeleine's beloved Cathedral of St. John the Divine that night; and those who wished to be there, but could not, were present in spirit, part of her community. Madeleine devoted her life and career to joy, peace, and love and brought these concepts into the lives of many, not only through her writing, but also through her workshops.

Thank you, Madeleine, for a lifetime of friendships. Without you, this never could have been. Now it is our duty to bring together the single drops of humanity into an ocean of community, to continue what Madeleine was trying to accomplish: creating communities, small pockets where joy, peace, and love continue to grow.

Madeleine L'Engle: Showing Us What it Means to be Human

by Peggy Harrington

Peggy Harrington, a poet and writer, served as Arts Coordinator at the Cathedral of St. John the Divine in New York, where she came to know Madeleine. A close friend of Madeleine and of many in Madeleine's circle, she died in November 2005. Peggy wrote the following piece as an introduction for one of the talks Madeleine gave at the Cathedral in December 1996. When she provided the piece for inclusion in a booklet celebrating Madeleine's eightieth birthday in 1996, Peggy related, "It says much of what is in my heart."

It is such an honor to stand here tonight to introduce to you a woman who, if you are like most of us, has already—through the spinning of her stories and reflections—transformed your lives in ways it would be difficult to recount.

How many of you have ever sat under the great dark bowl of heaven on a summer's night—on a rock, perhaps, still warm from the sun's caresses—and not felt the mystery and awe of Meg and Charles Wallace? Or have seen the glowing withers of a great unicorn in the cumulous of late spring? Have understood a little better the relationship of a star to an atom? Or the healing power of music? Have been taught how to love and to accept step-by-step life's mountains and molehills and her pitfalls, as well? How many have beheld a Biblical parable or story open to unexpected insights through eyes and ears new-formed through her guidance? Or have found the walk with a dying loved one made more bearable through Madeleine's words?

I don't know what combination of supreme luck and grace brought me here to the Cathedral and to the Community of the Holy Spirit so that I might grow to know and love this wonderful woman. I do know that her generosity has encouraged me, and so many others, to find our own spirits and voices. And has provided us with a community of friends and support such as I would have never dreamed possible in such a city. Somehow, some way, she gives us permission to cry, to laugh, to sing again. To be ourselves…

But we are gathered tonight to listen and to be filled, so I want to close with Madeleine's own words about stories and the tellers of tales.

"People have always told stories as they searched for truth. As our ancient ancestors sat around the campfire in front of their caves, they told the stories of their day in order to understand what their day had meant, what the truth of the mammoth hunt was, or the roar of the cave lion, or the falling in love of two young people. Bards and troubadours throughout the centuries have sung stories in order to give meaning to the events of human life.

". . . Jesus did not tell his parables in order to give us facts and information, but to show us truth . . .

"We tell stories, listen to stories, go to plays, to be amused, to be edified, but mostly so that we can understand what it means to be a human being."

I give you Madeleine L'Engle with thanks that she has so blessed my life—and yours. So that we can understand, more fully, what it means to be a human being.

Diane Amison, Isabelle Holland, Stephanie Cowell, Peggy Harrington, and Madeleine, around 1996.

Writing London, Writing Worcester County

by T. K. Hunter

Dr. T. K. Hunter is a historian, art historian, writer, consultant, public historian, and teacher at Columbia's Institute for Research in African-American Studies. She has presented numerous conference papers and written a number of book reviews and essays, including the essay "Geographies of Liberty" which appeared in Prophets of Protest *(New Press, 2006). Her history expertise centers on the English-speaking Black Atlantic in the seventeenth and eighteenth centuries, involving the movement of Blacks back and forth between Britain and the New World colonies. She took Madeleine's CHS workshop in the early 1990s.*

"Wild nights are my glory," Mrs Whatsit had declared with exuberance. I knew instinctively that when Madeleine L'Engle began *A Wrinkle in Time* with a storm, she offered to me, as a young astute reader, a literary joke: "it was a dark and stormy night"—the very phrase, canned and unimaginative (though it was suitably descriptive), that writers are supposed to avoid. I was drawn in not only because it was a compelling story but because someone had seen fit to feature kids (even if, by the time I had read *Wrinkle*, the slang was a bit quaint—charmingly so) and allow them to be in challenging situations where both their head and their heart were fully engaged. Madeleine's books had a richness to them, a recognition of the philosophical and moral complexities of a life well-lived and the fact that children could connect to those complexities. Indeed, her writing suggested that it was incumbent upon us to engage those intricacies. Quite simply, Madeleine's writing fed me and reinforced in me what I suspected at some level: that our challenge in life as human beings is to encounter and navigate the grey areas.

I continued to read other books by Madeleine, never dreaming for one moment that I would someday meet her, enroll in a writing workshop conducted by her, or have a casual conversation with her. Hold on to that conducting metaphor: Madeleine was instrumental in the development of my writing—my composition process—as well as in the belief in my ability to write.

I had come to Madeleine's workshop by accident. A few months before hearing of the workshop, after submitting a short story manuscript as my entry, I had been chosen by the author Gloria Naylor to be one of about twelve writers to participate in a day-long intensive Master Class she was giving; it was my first foray into the world of writing. But the Master Class—regardless of how flattering it was that Ms. Naylor had herself chosen my short story out of the numerous entries, and regardless of how intensive it was—was only for a day. And so, I was left to my own devices until my partner told me that he'd heard Madeleine L'Engle was holding a writing workshop of several weeks in length: the setting was to be small, and the class was not yet full.

Sanna Stanley, T. K. Hunter, Patricia McMahon, and Judith Lindbergh, during one of the writers' gatherings at 924 West End Ave.

For six weeks or so, we met regularly, gathered around a large, rectangular wooden table, and discussed writing: its glories, disciplines, frustrations, and pitfalls. We read what we produced, offered feedback, and Madeleine gave us assignments—some of which I thought were not only difficult, but, yes, I confess, a bit harebrained. (I would later come to know that Madeleine was many things but "harebrained" wasn't one of them!) I recall, particularly, sighing to myself when I heard Madeleine give one assignment: write a story from the standpoint of an animal—any animal, real or mythical. Great, I thought. That'll be really useful. I recall making several false starts: animal-lover though I am, I never felt a voice when I tried to write from the standpoint of an animal. I returned the following week empty-handed. Mind you, I was apologetic that I had nothing to share regarding the assignment, but I wasn't *overly* apologetic as I still did not like the assignment. Nevertheless, I tried to absorb the discussion about the stories that others had written.

Perhaps the listening and absorbing got me closer, perhaps not. It didn't get me closer immediately. But six months later, while staying in Whitby, England, hard by the North Yorkshire Moors, a pied wagtail visited a shallow puddle of water on the roof, just beyond my window . . . and a voice came to me. I began a vignette—it was too unformed to be classified as a short story, and remained so—and became fascinated by the life of that bird. The surprise wasn't that I was absorbed by such a creature (after all, when I was about twelve years old, I had been keen to become an ornithologist). Rather, it was that my resistance to a workshop exercise suggested by Madeleine took the better part of six months to dissipate. And when it did, something had clicked into place—a testament to the ways in which the subconscious works: quietly, diligently, unhurriedly. It is a fact for which writers are grateful. Madeleine had advocated such trust in one's subconscious, and enjoined us not to force things. This was the conductor saying *"softly, softly"* and "slowly, slowly." Following her lead, I saw the fruit of that wisdom six months later.

It was my writing group (formed the January after a number of us had finished Madeleine's winter workshop, and during the first of many annual dinner reunions in Madeleine's wonderful apartment) that heard the beginnings of my story about the pied wagtail. For more than ten years, my writing group was a central, stabilizing, dynamic force in my life. We functioned in a way that was (and remains today) rather unique where writers/writing workshops/writing programs are concerned, i.e., we did not use the group to work out our personal insecurities by allowing our egos to have free reign. This is not to say that we tiptoed around one another for years or decided that we would soft-pedal the truth; doing so would have certainly doomed our group and precipitated foundational cracks that would have quickly endangered our structural integrity. Rather, we agreed that the group would be a place where we would always respect one another, listen attentively, and offer considered, incisive criticism devoid of personal attack. In short, we understood our writers' group to be an oasis of the clear-eyed variety (as opposed to the rose-colored glasses variety). Our approach, our ethos was in many ways an important legacy of how Madeleine herself taught: with respect, with attentiveness, with criticism that was useful, as opposed to being an ego-booster for the one who offered it. As a result, we approached challenging situations (and there were a few of them) with all the patience, toughness, and understanding we could muster. And while those instances were fraught ones, we weathered them as a group, emerging with our abiding respect for one another intact.

In a talk I gave about a year ago (in my capacity as a history professor with a specialty in the eighteenth-century Afro-British Atlantic) to an audience at a national historic site—on African-Americans in the Revolutionary War Era—I offered a tribute (fond, poignant and knowing) to Madeleine. I began by noting that "every young writer is enjoined not to begin a story with the well-worn words 'It was a dark and stormy night.' But while I acknowledge that I learned that lesson well, I will begin tonight's talk, set in London in the early 1770s, thus: 'It was a dark and stormy night.'" I was rewarded with a satisfying ripple of laughter from the audience, and off I went to weave a true history tale of a windy night in November 1771, a ship bobbing at anchor in the Thames, a kidnapping, and English law. I'm sure Mrs Whatsit, too, was with me that evening in spirit.

Our lives have so many aspects: people come and go—intimates of the heart, and people less so. The mark they leave is like a gesture of paint: enter into the house of one's life, dip a finger into the bowl of paint by the door, and leave a sweep of color, a landscape, a self-portrait, a mural. There: that particular bright spot with the ripples extending outward a long way: that's the influence that Madeleine has had in my life from my discovery of her writing when I was a young geek-of-a-girl, to the writing workshop that it was my great good fortune to land in, to my writing group that formed out of it (where, in addition to my fiction work, I read conference papers and dissertation chapters), to my continuing professional writing. And while a reader of my professional history and law writing would not imagine in her wildest dreams that much of my writing ethic was shaped by Madeleine L'Engle, it is nevertheless true. The figures who I encounter in my work as a historian range across an ocean (the Atlantic) and wrestle internally with their allegiance (to the British in England who promise liberty, or to the American colonists who say they are fighting for it). They are the main characters in their own lives who clamor for me to tell their history, their story; and who sometimes—to that end—allow me to begin their tale of factual suspense by writing that the snows had receded in April 1781 in Worcester County, or to offer to an attentive audience waiting to hear about England and the law in 1771, the words, "It was a dark and stormy night."

Madeleine on the porch of Crosswicks, 1980s.

Balancing Art and Life

by Beth Vendryes Williams

Beth Vendryes Williams is an artist and art educator whose work is a metaphor for finding the holy in ordinary moments, people, places, and objects. Inspired by Madeleine's writings, she attended workshops at CHS in New York in the early 1990s. Her art is in many private collections throughout the country.

My journals from the time period in which I studied with Madeleine reflect my intense search for a way to hold onto the time and space I needed to create. I needed to find a way to allow the artist in me to flourish while I was nourishing a home and family. In addition, my art had evolved as a kind of visual prayer or meditation, and I was determined to maintain it. I hoped to find a solution that would enrich my family.

A trained artist and art educator, I worked as a kitchen designer for IKEA on the 2:00 to 10:00 p.m. shift and taught art part-time. Determined to make ends meet, my husband and I arranged our hours to cover care of our three young boys, ranging in age from five to nine. We lived in four rooms on the bottom floor of a one-family home, while we rented out the top floor. I sketched and painted daily, in between diaper changes, preparing dinner, cleaning, and helping with schoolwork. As you can imagine, I was having trouble finding time and energy to work as an artist. My husband was fully supportive, but I was feeling frustrated juggling work, my creative career, my family, and finances.

Then, by chance, I came across some of Madeleine's writings and felt she was empathetic to my plight. Out of the blue, an intuitive cousin called me to tell me there was a Madeleine L'Engle workshop at CHS in New York. Inspired to take her class by her books, I signed up for the workshop despite my lack of writing experience. I had come to the realization that I needed to find a way to effectively combine my passions. Now I was in need of advice. I needed a mentor for balancing creativity, spirituality, and family.

As several workshop participants, friends, and I strolled out under the street lamps after the first evening writing workshop, I saw Madeleine, rushed to catch up with her, and tugged on her sleeve, asking for her suggestions for finding a way to balance it all. After all, I felt I had to "seize the day"! This quest for balance was what motivated me to drive into New York City on a Monday night. I had never driven into the city before! I would not allow this opportunity to pass me by.

"I have been juggling my artwork, my growing family, and working. I know from your books that you've managed to find the time for writing and relationships, with stability and balance in your life. Is there anything you can tell me that will help me to create equilibrium? How do you do it?" I asked Madeleine. "Can I find that peace? Is there hope? Is it possible to find the time to create, or am I doing a disservice to my family and to my artwork?"

Oh, how she loved speaking with me that night about juggling it all! I told her how I worked with beeswax crayons and watercolor to keep the work non-toxic. I worked in my journal, documenting daily life with the boys, but was having trouble doing art consistently. She was willing to discuss issues rarely articulated in my conversations with artists before. She also took the time to look directly in my eyes and listen from her heart. She insisted that I trust my instincts and listen to my own work. That was my biggest job. To listen ... and to paint what I heard and saw in my mind's eye. The complex richness of my life would provide material for my work. She exhorted me to keep on working regularly.

I went home basking in the affirmation that my art was my prayer. As her writings said, I could believe that "Our truest responsibility to the irrationality of the world is to paint or sing or write, for only in such response do we find the truth."

She explained, in later classes, that she wrote books when her children were little and her husband was working as an actor. She encouraged us to work every day, even for a short time, taking every opportunity to write.

So began the transformative writing workshop experiences with Madeleine. Slowly each piece of my work became more connected to the next. I made sure my art materials were entirely transportable in a large flexible pocketbook. I sketched while waiting for appointments, to entertain the children, when we were waiting for a tow truck, when they were napping. I painted laundry fresh from the dryer or line, before I folded it! I sometimes left the dishes in the sink until five minutes before I had to prepare dinner and my husband came home. My boys were always encouraged to play, make up their own stories, read, and draw quietly, and I developed the ability to stop and start work without despairing, knowing that my ritual of creating was my vocation and would always be there when the boys' momentary needs were resolved.

I strained to catch every nuance of Madeleine's conversations in the workshops, applying the words to my visual work. She encouraged us to provide ourselves with a regular opportunity to create work each day, whether we were inspired or not. I found myself writing in a stream-of-consciousness technique alongside my drawing and painting.

I began to settle into driving into the city for these workshops. There were some little adventures, however. Driving past the Upper West Side into the Bronx, heading toward Yankee Stadium, contributed to lateness in one class. Tollbooths were always a challenge. Back then, you had to have exact change! Giving Madeleine a ride to her city apartment along with another workshop member and friend, whom I had recruited for this adventure, turned into a rodeo ride when I naively parked in a narrow lot surrounded by buildings on three sides. I saw the gate blocking the driveway but didn't know it would be locked after 10:00 pm. "Don't worry," I assured her, "we will get out of here in one piece!" I proceeded to do a series of pirouettes on three-point turns to redirect the car toward my only outlet. We held our breaths while one set of wheels rode on the sidewalk, which was not blocked by the gate, while the other rolled lower at street level, and we just squeezed by the gate onto the street, all three of us screaming! Madeleine exclaimed at my wild and adventurous spirit and was grateful for the exciting and ultimately safe ride home. I was thankful that I didn't scratch the car or destroy the suspension system.

As the workshops progressed, I had more questions, of course. I took two or three classes consecutively. Although the writing medium was different from my usual tools of paint and drawing pencil, I found the concerns, problems, and solutions to be translatable from words to paint. A workshop atmosphere of empathy, caring, interest in issues concerning creativity, self-discipline, inspiration, stretching oneself, and finding balance was fostered. Madeleine was a natural teacher, encouraging and intolerant of artifice. She believed in each of us as incredibly creative beings, capable of whatever we set our minds and hearts to. In her words, "Creativity is a way of living, no matter what our vocation or how we earn a living."

I began to trust in my abilities to articulate my stories and ideas. This was a valuable insight, because I had lacked clarity and confidence in my writing. The process of writing ideas and stories broke through invisible boundaries into my visual imagination, and I found myself attempting methods such as adapting the use of "midrash" (a commentary explanation or illustration of a concept found in scripture) to tell stories in my paintings and drawings.

I understood that I should approach my work as a ritual that served to catch the inspiration when it passed through my soul. I was astonished to read her words in *Walking on Water*: "To work on a book is for me very much the same thing as to pray. Both involve discipline. If the artist works only when he feels like it, he's not apt to build up much of a body of work."

Before I took the workshops, the connection between creating and praying was something I had always felt, yet had not affirmed. I began to infuse my daily routine with a regularly scheduled time to draw in my journal and paint, even when I was not feeling inspired. Madeleine shares her thoughts on the connection between prayer and writing in detail in *Walking on Water*. Reading the book, I wondered if I could make work that shares the essence of my spirituality without constantly making specific religious references. Was my vocation to make art about ordinary people, places, and events that are holy in themselves?

Madeleine talked to us about allowing ourselves to "listen" to our work. Perceiving the voice within required us to allow the experience of *Kairos*, or God's time, as opposed to *Chronos*, or clock time. This could give us the space to listen to God. Therefore, creating, whether it is writing or drawing, and reflecting on it, could give us the time and space to listen and respond to God—to pray. She spoke to us about angels, how awesomely powerful they are and even terrifying in their beauty and strength. Again, she made an affirmation of visible symbols of spiritual being. I have since explored the presence of angels in a pivotal painting in my work.

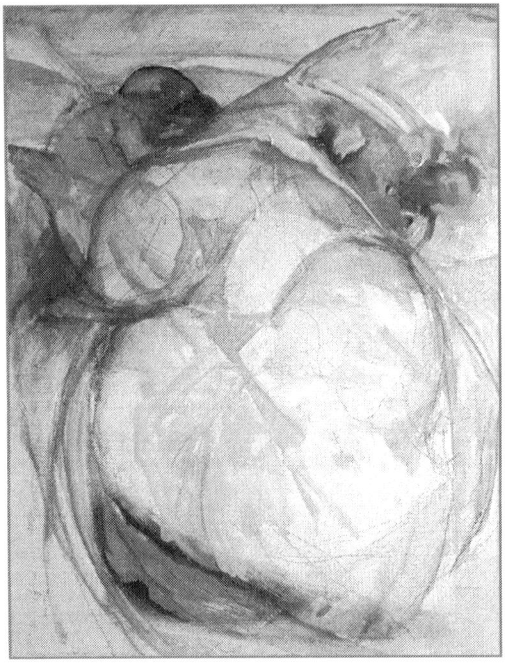

Guardian by Beth Vendryes Williams, oil on canvas, 2005.

Sixteen years later, I am still transforming myself with the understandings that broke into my consciousness because of Madeleine's workshops and writings. Each day I arise at 4:00 a.m. to meditate and paint. I leave for work as an elementary art educator at 7:00 a.m. I teach my 600 students that "every mistake is an opportunity to create something new." I remind them (and myself!) that "the energy to create goes from the eyes to the head to the heart to the hands to the paper." I discipline myself to leave work at a reasonable time, walk and do yoga for energy, and read books and work on the entrepreneurial part of being an artist after dinner. My children? The boys are now young men who consider it a priority to make a difference in the world, each in his own unique way. My husband is thrilled that I continue to pursue my work. My practice also gives him the chance to explore his own creativity through gardening, photography, and writing. Having just had a show of work based on the "liturgy of hours" as a way of structuring our waking hours, I explore the day visually in terms of light and time.

As I wrote this essay, I became aware of just how much grace I received as a participant in Madeleine's workshops. Her references to art and spirituality continue to remind me of ways to be true to my spirit in my art. Her attitude and determination persist in motivating me. Her ability to share her insights has enriched both my art and my life, and I now understand, after all, that one is a reflection of the other. Ordinary daily life, consequently, offers me an opportunity to uncover the spirit, and make it perceptible in my work.

Thank you, Madeleine.

Madeleine L'Engle: Apostle of the Word

by Janet O'Connell

Janet O'Connell took CHS workshops with Madeleine L'Engle in the early 1990s. She has combined creative writing with positions in teaching, inner city missionary work, and day care management. She continues to pursue writing as she leads a community writers' group in the Adirondack Mountains in upstate New York.

> "I could go on and on picking out passages of God's love, God's mercy, God's forgiveness, but . . . I knew that I was alive because of God's love. I knew that God would show me why my life had been spared and would let me know what I was supposed to do. One thing I never lost was faith in God's love."
>
> —Madeleine L'Engle, *The Rock That Is Higher*

I first met Madeleine in her emotion-packed book *The Rock That Is Higher.* The book opens with Madeleine far away from home, severely injured, and on her way to a hospital. There had been a horrible crash when a truck driver ran a red light. The injured author captured my affection in the first five pages, because I had experienced the loss of a brother in a tragic automobile accident where six people were killed. I would relate personally and sympathetically to every chapter—every sentence—in this book.

During Madeleine's battle of the senses in the shadow of death, she was highly aware of her intense pain and frightening vulnerability. She pleaded at death's threshold that God would let her die quickly, as she struggled with troubling questions and the darkness of anger and aloneness. But then the glimmers of hope, which she spoke of as "deep, innate faith," rose to the surface and restored her courage and determination. I have no doubt that God revealed to her why her life was spared; surely this book is reason enough.

The Scriptures that Madeleine explored in the writing of *Rock*, seeking spiritual direction and solace, are my favorite Bible stories. This book brought refreshing new insights to them. I was moved by her discernment of forgiveness as a gift of God's grace and heartened at the comfort she gained from that confidence. The book is her journey through pain, grief, and healing, which culminates in her revived enjoyment of the sweet fruits of her stalwart faith—so beautifully expressed in the quote above. Joy is indeed the sweetest fruit, which she shares with us in the marvelous devotional chapter "Story as Joy" (Chapter 8). I highly recommend the book for personal and small-group devotional study.

Madeleine's deep spiritual aspect and her contemplation of the mysteries and paradoxes of faith are foundational in her portraits of Biblical characters. These portraits abound in her book of poems, *A Cry Like a Bell.* The poems show Madeleine's profound empathy with suffering, conflict, and doubt; and then—*wham*—they climax in trust, joy and praise. For Advent and Lenten programs, I have presented many of her poems, and the worshipers keep asking for more. This has led to sharing my own poems as well. It's been a marvelous experience.

Rock was a blessing to me during a time of perplexity and struggle, but it was *Walking on Water* that gave me the "shot in the arm" I needed to do more and better work at something I love: creative writing. Somewhere in the book, Madeleine gave an example of a writing exercise she taught in seminars. I stopped reading, took up a pen, and wrote for an hour. After writing my first sentence, "I was leaning forward into the busy street, when a gentle tug at my collar pulled me. . ." I was off and running with a delightful little story that I had no idea was tucked away in my mental filing cabinet. I could hardly believe it! But it was just what she said might happen.

The books were all I needed to love the author, but I was thrilled when my friend Pamela Leggett (who had introduced me to her books) brought me to my first writers' workshop with Madeleine. Walking into the convent, the Community of the Holy Spirit, was itself a delightful experience. Blessed quiet in the midst of uptown Manhattan, aromas of home cooking, smiling nuns in black habits, and the lilt of gentle evensong were nearly mesmerizing. I'm sure I was a happy face when someone said, "May I introduce you to Madeleine L'Engle?" Little did I know that over time, I would be driving her home after classes and would have the opportunity to get to know her as a personal friend as well as the b-e-s-t writer's mentor.

When I look back over two to three decades, I cannot imagine "me" without knowing Madeleine. I am so grateful for her loving affirmation and encouragement to write what I believe. I can still see her sitting in her favorite chair in the living room of her New York City apartment, elbows on the chair's arms, hands folded, nodding her head slowly, when I said, "Madeleine, God has again faced me with another poem, and I just love it!"

"I know," Madeleine said, "I know!"

I remember fondly the community of writers I came to know through the workshops. Many of them may remember the following experience, which led to one of Madeleine's extraordinary assignments. Frequently, a number of us would go to the convent for Vespers and supper before the workshop. One stormy evening as we sat in the basement enjoying delicious hot soup, there was a sudden, startling crash at a window. Everyone gasped and stared in the direction of the window. Within seconds, Madeleine stood up and said, "Okay, everyone, here's your assignment for next week. Someone was killed in this room. Write about it."

The refrain of a ballad called "Who Killed Sister Madeleine?" was racing through my mind before my head hit the pillow that night. For me, it's a portrait of the Madeleine I was gifted to know: witty, whimsical, determined, deeply spiritual, aware of angels, loving and dearly loved.

The ballad begins with this refrain:

Who killed Sister Madeleine
with a smile upon her face
until we solve this mystery
no one leaves this place

I go on to describe the shock and horror of the convent sisters at the untimely death (by pen) of their dear friend:

Ah, we will tell you what we know
the Sister Agnes sobbed
she loved her dresses long and full
preferred her grey locks bobbed

She knew the style had long since changed
and she should show some leg
but she wouldn't listen to a priest
much less to Sister Peg

Others said she cooked and baked
but wouldn't scrub a pan
we tried to show her how it's done
but she just up and ran

She gave her students half an hour
a masterpiece to write
she wouldn't budge one tiny inch
if one put up a fight

The reader never finds out who killed the Sister named Madeleine, but we see her departure for heaven. There's a rush of wind in the room, and a radiant cherub swirls in and lands on Madeleine's arm:

He gave a whistle like a cop
and raised one fluttering wing
he held her cross medallion high
and asked them all to sing

He led a song about a child
who with his crayon red
colored Madeleine white as snow
and to His father said

Receive today this holy one
this daughter now reclaim
long since You chose her as your own
and called her by a name

The sisters reached to say good-bye
tear-stained and arms stretched wide
she with the sprite ascended high
to greet the heavenly side!

Who killed Sister Madeleine
it happened in this place
she left us with God's cherubim
a smile upon her face!

Whether by cherubim or chariot, Madeleine is in heaven! No doubt about it. With radiant face and folded hands (ah, me, did she take that armchair with her?), she sings Bach anthems and plays duets with Mozart. Playfully kicking up heaps of dried words along a golden path, she strolls with Dietrich Bonhoeffer and Martin Luther as the sages discuss costly grace and justification by faith. Madeleine is in her glory, glorifying the God of unspeakable wonders.

The Rock That Is Higher is all about story as Madeleine journeys through an extremely difficult time of suffering, but the foundational cornerstone of this great book is resurrection. Madeleine had experienced rebirth of body and spirit through God's love and mercy. Abounding in the renewed joy of faith, Madeleine concludes this book with four of the most significant words in the Christian lexicon: He is Risen Indeed! Amen, Madeleine, Amen!

Pamela Leggett, Janet O'Connell holding Pam's daughter, Krista, and Madeleine, October 1995.

An Open Window to God

by Sally Lowe Whitehead

Sally Lowe Whitehead is the author of The Truth Shall Set You Free: A Family's Passage from Fundamentalism to a New Understanding of Faith, Love, and Sexual Identity. *She took several writing of Madeleine's writing workshops beginning in 1991.*

"An icon is an open window to God."

—Madeleine L'Engle, Holy Cross Monastery, January 1991

I fell under the enchantment of Madeleine L'Engle's writing—and eventually under the enchantment of the lady extraordinaire herself—probably later than most. I was thirty-two years old when I read *A Wrinkle in Time.* While my husband drove our seven children back to our log house in the North Georgia hills from my parents' home, I was completely engrossed in the story of a brilliant family caught in a mysterious phenomenon called a "tesseract" and their exceedingly courageous feats of love.

The breadth and depth of Madeleine's first book of fiction stirred a quiescent longing for spiritual mystery and mysticism I'd mostly managed to deny myself. For ten years my family had been deeply entrenched in heavy duty Christian fundamentalism and an inexorable view of God. I had begun to grow weary of it all. Apparently lacking an acceptably submissive spirit, I'd been sorely rebuked by those "in authority" over me (who included my husband, our pastor, and his elders) for questioning God or for seeking more experiences of God than were deemed permissible. They were there to teach me all I needed to know about God. My sins were considered serious, and it appeared I was unrepentant and a habitual offender. I knew reading *A Wrinkle in Time* teetered on the edge of heresy. Regardless, I could not put it down.

I was relieved that, despite almost overwhelming fear and trepidation, Michael and I'd begun to loosen our spiritual reins. What I did not know then, as we drove on silently, lost in our own thoughts, was that Michael's reasons for doing so predominantly stemmed from a closely guarded secret held in a sickening internal grip. It would be seven years before he would finally feel safe enough to release his secret to me, after which the world as we knew it would forever cease to be. Thankfully, no, mercifully, Madeleine L'Engle would be there again to help me. And, miraculously, I would receive her compassionate counsel in person.

Madeleine L'Engle's book had presented me with a new and much-needed perspective with which to consider God. Though a work of fiction, it had enlarged my view of possible goings-on in the vast universe created and sustained by God. In the book, evil was present and powerful but, as terribly frightening as it was for the characters in the story to be caught in an unknown spiritual realm, each time evil deceived or hurt them the enormous power of love *always* prevailed. This was a revolutionary notion for me to consider, as the dogma we had adhered to insisted on a literal Satan and a very real Hell.

> "Que la terre est petite *a qui la voit des cieux!* De Lille.
> (How small is the earth to him who looks from heaven.)"
>
> —Mrs Who, *A Wrinkle in Time*

It would be years before I'd be liberated entirely from the fear of being deceived by my heart (which I'd been taught never to trust) or by "false teachers" (who were ready to prey on those who dared to stray from the fold). Yet, while reading *A Wrinkle in Time,* I'd come upon possibilities about God that both surprised and delighted me. Though unaware of it, I was close to experiencing the real power and truth in Christ's assurance that "You shall know the truth and the truth shall set you free." (John 8:32)

Within four months of that trip to my parents' home in St. Simon's Island, my sixty-seven-year-old mother became desperately ill and died. I understood then the urgency I'd suddenly felt to ask my husband to make the long trip. After her death, I railed at God in anger and confusion. I ached over the gross and indignant sufferings she had been forced to endure, and I grieved—sometimes inconsolably—over the impossible reality of being motherless. It was from another of Madeleine's books that I gleaned solace, compassion, and affirmation.

> "I sometimes get very angry at God and I do not feel guilty about it, because the anger is an affirmation of faith. *You cannot get angry at someone who is not there."*
>
> —Madeleine L'Engle, *The Irrational Season*

Even more important, as I read, I understood that perhaps what I'd been taught about God's judgment and wrath (especially reserved for those, like my mother, who were presumed "unsaved" as determined by our fundamentalist teachers' literal interpretation of the Bible) was perhaps not so "written in stone." It seemed there might be gentler, more redemptive possibilities than a one-way ticket to hell. Through Madeleine's words, I'd clearly found a window of hope.

> "No one should be refused at God's table. God does not need our protection. When we start feeling the need to protect God, we're in trouble."
>
> —Madeleine L'Engle, Holy Cross Monastery, January 1991

By 1990, Michael and I had completed the physical exodus out of extreme fundamentalism and returned to the comparatively liberal "promised land" of the Episcopal Church. I had continued to read every Madeleine L'Engle book I could get my hands on and, feeling I might want to try my own hand at writing, had begun taking writing classes at a local arts center. Gradually I let go of the idea that I had to have all the right answers to my spiritual questions. I began to grant myself the freedom both to think and say, "I'm not sure" and to actually believe God would not turn His back on me in fiery retribution. Slowly but surely, I was developing something that had previously terrified me—an open mind.

> "What God made, God will complete."
>
> —Madeleine L'Engle

Life was less grueling, more joyful, sometimes even exciting, yet ghostly fears and debilitating bouts of self-doubt haunted me every step of the way. I also had a persistently nagging belief that my husband and I were not, shall we say, "on the same page" in our marriage. He angrily suggested that any problems we had were mine, not his. Though supposedly liberated from years of attempted wifely submission, unfortunately, I still assumed him to be right. Craving advice, I often read excerpts from a poem by Madeleine in *The Irrational Season*:

> "Because you're not what I would have you be
> I blind myself to who, in truth, you are."

The poem goes on to suggest that by refusing to see and accept a loved one honestly we impair our ability to see in him, or her, a reflection of God. I prayed with all my heart that I could experience this sort of nonjudgmental love with my husband. All prayers are answered, though often in ways we could never imagine. Eventually I would find this place with Michael, but it would little resemble what I had imagined.

I wrote Madeleine a letter about my mother's death, our turbulent exodus from fundamentalism, some of my irksome fears and doubts, and my growing desire to write. She graciously answered and suggested I attend one of her upcoming writers' workshops, in January 1991. Still beleaguered by what I believed was an inability to discern truth from a lie, I nevertheless threw caution to the wind and registered for Madeleine's three-day writers' workshop and three-day silent spiritual retreat at Holy Cross Monastery in West Park, New York. Still uncertain the voice of my own heart could be could trusted, I'd rarely listened to and therefore barely recognized it. It was beyond time to learn to do so.

> "Be willing to live in a world where questions are more important than answers. Learn to live with 'cosmic insecurity'!"
>
> —Madeleine L'Engle, Holy Cross Monastery, January 1991

The first time I'd seen Madeleine L'Engle was at a book signing in Memphis, Tennessee. This was a few years before my journey to Holy Cross. Along with a couple of friends, I had heard her speak, then shyly asked her to sign my book. It had been a wonderful, magical night, and her talk had significantly inspired me.

Now, on the morning of our first writing class, my experience was altogether different. I was kneeling in the Holy Cross chapel, waiting for service to begin, when like a true wind in the door, I felt her presence before I saw her. When I dared look up, she had indeed breezed past me, leaving behind what felt like a mother's touch on the cheek or perhaps a father's welcome-home embrace. She joined the monks in their choir stall. Attired in an elegant black velvet hooded cloak, she looked positively regal. I held my breath until I saw her smile and nod hello to us all. In unison, we rose to sing. Dizzy with the wonder of what felt like truly sacred space, *with her*, knowing days like this stretched out before me, I could barely see the words on my hymnal page for my embarrassing tears of joy.

> "Every action of love makes a cosmic difference. When we respond with fear and hate, it does too. *Joy is the infallible sign of the presence of God.*"
>
> —Madeleine L'Engle

I had arrived at Holy Cross with a powerful sense of urgency to get on with what, all things considered, I had decided was a seriously interrupted life. I was totally aware of how different I was from the other attendees. Probably I was the least formally educated, the only recovering fundamentalist, the most novice writer, and the only Southerner in the bunch. But I could hardly wait to immerse myself in the wisdom pool available to me there for six full days and nights. I wanted to meet each of the incredibly stimulating people gathered around Madeleine and hear their stories. Consequently, I lingered in conversations to the very last minute, though rarely contributing a single word. Silently, I vowed that, when the time came, I would do my best to study alongside this passionate group of "real writers" with as little self-deprecation as possible.

When class began, I was surprised at the atmosphere of warmth and safety. I would come to know this was the norm in Madeleine's classes and workshops. She urged writers who ranged from the prolifically published to "newbies" like myself to be serious about their work, yet she insisted that critiques spoken out loud should always be delivered in a spirit of gentle helpfulness. While I was completely happy to just BE in a room full of such bright stars, clearly all were equally willing and ready to soak up every word of her instructions.

> "Write with heart, not sentimentality. If you're in tears over a scene, it should be in the garbage. You're listening to self, not story."
>
> —Madeleine L'Engle

After a while she sent us to our cells to take a Bible story and rewrite it from another character's perspective. (For example, in the story of Cain and Abel, try writing it from Cain's perspective, perhaps telling why he did what he did.) Reading our minds as we drifted unhurriedly out the door, she firmly added, "How do we *ever* know what we write will be of value to anyone else? Stories have to be believable; they don't have to be possible. Write anything that comes to mind to prime the pump. *Inspiration comes while you're doing it!*"

A discipline called "The Great Silence" was strictly observed by the monks every night from the evening service known as Compline through the next day's breakfast, and was therefore followed by the visiting writers as well. This practice helped to gently ease me into the silence of the spiritual retreat that began the same day the workshop ended. The only human voice participants heard for the next three days of retreat was Madeleine's as she intermittently read and taught from her new book, *The Glorious Impossible.* And, not surprisingly, her teachings had a familiar theme: letting go of fear and doubt.

> "Humans are the only creatures allowed to experience failure. We are human beings because we fail. We make mistakes to learn. My greatest challenge right now is learning not to judge those who judge!"
>
> —Madeleine L'Engle, Holy Cross Monastery, January 1991

Up to that point, *silence* had not always been my friend. My mother, fragmented and sometimes lost in her own depression-hell, had masterfully used silence as punishment. Silence was the outcome of her sudden, unexplained anger and could mean hours, days, even weeks of estrangement. Silence was therefore something to be avoided, not sought. Madeleine would be the first, though not the last, teacher to urge me into the silence where the Divine I longed to know resided.

> "Entering into silence is like going to the ocean. At first you dabble in it. When you look out and see the dolphins playing, you know it's safe to go out into the deep."
>
> —Madeleine L'Engle, Holy Cross Monastery, January 1991

Traveling to Holy Cross Monastery to study writing at the feet of a most brilliant and prolific author like Madeleine L'Engle was obviously an act of over-the-top audacity. But the pure and simple truth of it was: I had to. In my heart I carried a particularly strong wish. Having read everything I could about Madeleine's faith journey, I believed she could guide me across the harrowing border at which I stood, where behind me lay the fear-based spirituality of my past, and ahead lay the mysterious unknown and the spiritual freedom I desperately sought.

> "Take a chance on the impossible being possible!"
>
> —Madeleine L'Engle, Holy Cross Monastery, January 1991

As it turned out, Madeleine made herself available to any student desiring private counseling sessions. Mustering up all my bravery, I requested a session, to which she agreed. We talked for more than an hour, and my pain seemed to be reflected on her face. Her strong words of reassurance and encouragement reached the very depth of my being. ("YES! Keep going, you're on the right path. You're not being deceived. And even if you are, you will learn to know it. YES! Trust your heart. You will not remain full of fear and doubt; avail yourself to God and your fears will slowly subside. YES! Be gentle with Michael.") Neither of us knew that the road she urged me to trust and travel that day would be a most terrifying one, but one that would ultimately lead me exactly where I needed to be.

"Why don't you come to the fall workshop and retreat?" Madeleine asked when our talk was over. "It will be at the Community of the Holy Spirit's convent in Brewster, New York, called Melrose. Being with the nuns is a totally different experience and one I believe you will also enjoy." My answer of course was a resounding "yes."

By the end of the week, I found that the ritual of silence had indeed become my friend. Sitting at breakfast, or with others in the library as we quietly read and wrote, I felt at peace and unified—never alone or afraid. All too soon our time with Madeleine ended. When I approached her to offer my goodbye and thanks, she opened her arms wide and enfolded me for several long minutes. Words, I found, were unnecessary.

> "In the most acute pain, we stumble into the most incredible joy."
>
> —Madeleine L'Engle

Two months before I was to return to New York for the fall workshop and retreat, my husband of twenty-one years finally broke down from the weight of his long-held secret and told me the truth: he was and always had been a gay man hiding behind a well-kept straight life. He adored his children and loved me. We both began to understand that continuing our marriage, after knowing the truth, would not only be living a lie but denying us the chance for an authentic life. The hardest part was figuring out how to actually dismantle our large family. Survival often seemed questionable, yet the only possible way was to go through the pain.

I wrote to Madeleine. I told her only that I had discovered a serious problem existed with Michael, asked for her prayers, and asked if I could possibly talk to her at Melrose in November. Too, I thanked her for "being an icon for me... enabling me to stretch and soften my heart," knowing that she had unwittingly prepared me for this time in my life.

November finally came, and I departed for what would be my second workshop and retreat with Madeleine, feeling nothing like the curious young woman I'd been only a year before. This time, my heart was heavy with mixed emotions and my head was full of much confusion. Before my plane landed in New York, I experienced a slight break in the darkness incessantly clouding over me. Encouraged, I asked God if I could step outside of my life just long enough to gain the clarity I so desperately needed. Could I just be ME, not someone's mother or wife or daughter-in-law or whomever else... but just me, for just this week? I believed, in my heart, I heard a quiet but firm "yes."

"Sometimes rules are broken for love. Jesus was far more concerned with love than with judgment."

—Madeleine L'Engle, Melrose: The Convent, November 1991

While in New York City I attended the Community of the Holy Spirit's weekly community Sunday supper at St. Hilda's House, so I could meet the city sisters before going to the country convent, Melrose, for Madeleine's workshop. There, I was introduced to a man visiting from California named Mel, with whom—after talking for several hours that evening—I spent the next few days touring the city. It quickly became apparent we were attracted to each other. Had I lost my mind? Perhaps, yet somehow, it felt beautifully and gracefully right.

All too soon it was time to head to Melrose—and, at last, to my dear Madeleine. Though it was hard saying goodbye to the tall, handsome man I'd met and enjoyed time with, but doubted I'd ever see again, I boarded the train for Melrose anxious to hear Madeleine's advice.

Not long after I arrived, Madeleine called me to her bedroom for counseling. Trying hard to control my emotions so I could speak, I began to explain the *real* reason for my crumbling marriage, how hard we'd tried to figure out a way to stay together, and how we'd finally begun to see the errors in that way of thinking. Finally, I confided a little about the man I'd met in New York and my confusingly amorous feelings. While I was still talking, Madeleine abruptly stopped me and said, "You don't have a mother do you?"

Surprised, I wondered if she remembered the letter I'd written her years ago, and shyly answered, "No, my mother died about eight years ago."

"I thought so," she said. "Come here. You need a lap."

And so it was, I spent the next forty-five minutes talking, listening, and crying as needed, all the while held securely in Madeleine's broad lap. When I had finally talked my way through and she had told me many wise things (including that she had given me a roommate who had also gone through "deep shit" and that we should talk), we hugged and I reluctantly slid down to leave.

"Wait," she said, and picked up a piece of paper, quickly scribbled something down, and handed it to me. "Call me," she said firmly. "Anytime."

Outside her door, I opened my hand to see what she had written. On the slip of paper, which I still have to this day, were Madeleine's two private phone numbers. I slowly closed my hand over what felt like purest gold. Once home, I never had to make that call, but just knowing I could was enough to hang on to through some of the most excruciating days and nights I would ever have to endure. The longest and darkest ones were when my children had to face the truth about their parents' inability to remain married, and the oldest ones had to face the real reason. To this day, when I think about that time, I'm reminded of an indescribable, almost unbearable pain—one I thank God we have all finally moved beyond.

> "We forgive. God, however, not just forgives, but forgets. You may always remember the wrong, but when you can remember and not feel the pain, you have forgiven."
>
> —Madeleine L'Engle, Melrose: The Convent, November 1991

By spring our amicable divorce was final and Michael and I both were moving on with our separate lives. In January, 1992, I, along with two of my sons, made a major move to New York City. Two of my other sons stayed with their father; the two oldest were, by then, out of the house. (As difficult as it was for us, the seventh child, a mentally and physically handicapped girl our family had fostered for eight years, had to be sent to live with another family.) Life had been turned upside down and shaken. It would never look or feel the same.

I, too, had changed in just about every way imaginable from the tremendously sheltered, fearful woman who in 1984 had read *A Wrinkle in Time* to a far more confident one who had rediscovered the voice of her heart. As mentor, Madeleine taught me many things, not the least of which was to consider the Divine feminine along with the masculine. A true feminist, she often said women were falsely viewed as either "nurturers or devourers" and should rid themselves of "unnecessary shame and guilt." More than once I heard her remind her female students that we were "killing ourselves by trying to live up to impossible, plastic images," adding that, "if an image is not loving, it is not God." Madeleine introduced me to the feminine aspect of God which has continued to be the focus of my personal spirituality, something else for which I owe her an eternal debt of gratitude.

> "Don't get hung up on literalism—it's the great crippler. In the French Bible, the Gospel of John has God as feminine."
>
> —Madeleine L'Engle, Holy Cross Monastery, January 1991

Every day I marveled at the simple reality of *living* in the city, and despite the painful losses my family and I had incurred, I was grateful for the tremendous good we had come to know. One particular "good" shone brightly in my life, and still does to this day. Mel, the man I'd met at the Community of the Holy Spirit convent a year before, had become the love of my life, and in the spring of 1993, we became engaged.

I worked at Pottery Barn during the day and took evening writing classes with Madeleine, during which I met many a fantastic writer and befriended a few. Occasionally I had the pleasure of walking with Madeleine from her apartment to St. John the Divine's library, where she often went to write, and we would talk. I relished those times with her. She met and embraced my two young sons, and as I saw their faces light up, I offered a silent thank you to God. I enjoyed several impromptu piano concerts on her baby grand, played by both Mel and Madeleine. Occasionally she would ask Mel to help with a task around the house. Madeleine liked Mel very much and, thankfully, approved of our relationship. Since he was very tall, wonderfully handsome, and a dignified stage performer of opera, though not of theater, I often wondered if Mel didn't remind Madeleine a bit of her beloved Hugh.

It was apparent Madeleine thrived on regular visits from her many adoring students and friends. Never, it seemed, did she tire from our questions and requests regarding writing or spirituality. She was quite candid about her need for people, saying, "It's a big breakthrough when we can be honest and say 'please stay' when we're inclined to say, 'I'm okay, you can go.'" She also insisted that "Humans are far harder on themselves than God ever is."

Many lively spiritual discussions sprang up spontaneously amongst us. Despite her loving attitude and teachings of non-judgment, Madeleine had very strong opinions about right and wrong. And, to my initial horror, I did not always agree. So great was my respect for and devotion to her, I found this discovery difficult, and yet I knew if I sought to emulate this strong woman, I could not revert back to my days of unequal submission. It became then my task to learn to allow Madeleine to be fully human—as perfect in her imperfections—just as she had encouraged me and others.

There was one particular time when Madeleine's opinion was not the right one for me. An incredible opportunity to write and probably publish my memoir came along—about the most wonderful news I could imagine. I had talked to my former husband, Michael, who encouraged me to write my story (including "our story") in total honestly with the hope it would help others find the courage to face their own truths. While Madeleine believed it would be good and cathartic for me to write my story, she emphatically stated it was not appropriate to write or publish it as nonfiction. I was stunned. I thought she'd be thrilled—even proud. I worried that she didn't think I was a good enough writer. Then I angrily wondered if she was afraid of what others might think. Finally, I sighed and asked her to please explain.

"Because," she said, "you just cannot write the truth about this. It wouldn't be right."

"Yes, Madeleine, I believe I not only can but will," I replied, hoping my voice sounded as strong as my conviction. I waited for her to continue but she was silent. She looked pensive, even sad, and then her expression shifted to an unfamiliar, stony look. She never fully explained her reasoning and never wavered in her opinion. Nor did I probe. I understood and respected her right to make those choices, and I also understood the reasons for making mine.

As radical, even wrong, as it seemed to her, I vowed to tell the truth as best I could, without flagrantly causing harm, to bring all my family and I had experienced to the attention of a larger audience. This was how change would come about, part of how we evolved. And when it came to fundamentalism, sexual identity issues, and a new understanding of love and family, in my opinion, evolution was certainly needed.

Whether it was a generational breach we simply could not traverse, or something more personal, I will never know. In the end, we lovingly agreed to disagree, and she wished me well. It was clear I would have to write my story without her genuine approval or, I imagined, her guidance—both of which pained me greatly. Nonetheless, I had to do what my heart told me was right. In fact, Madeleine never allowed this matter to intrude upon our relationship; we simply continued as if it were not happening. In the end, she offered as generous and gracious congratulations as I'm sure was possible, by writing a warm endorsement for the book's jacket.

Each memory of Madeleine is priceless, and each one seems to beget another, so I must now force myself to stop. There is, however, one more, best related by a journal note I wrote on January 18, 1994:

> Tonight I took dinner to Madeleine's apartment. She had knee surgery on December 29th and is doing well. A lady named Marilyn from Michigan is staying with her and her friend Barbara arrived about 8:00 PM. And so we all ate together. I really enjoyed Barbara. She writes for Bishop Browning. Throughout the evening, Madeleine had me relate what she called the "Mel and Sally story." It was quite fun. Then we talked about our upcoming wedding! Someone asked who was "giving me away" or, as I like to put it, "presenting me." I decided to go ahead and tell Madeleine that my first and only heart response was—her! From her bed, she announced, "I will, Sally!" I protested, "But you can't, what about your knee?!" To which she retorted, "I CAN and I

WILL. I'll be fine by then and I can walk you down the aisle with my cane." Then she proceeded—to the shrieks of us all—to prove her agility by getting OUT of the bed, walking around the house in her walker, then coming down the long hall leaning on her cane! Madeleine L'Engle really is presenting me to Mel Whitehead at our wedding on February 5th! I am in awe of how this is all working out. . . .

And so it was, Mel and I were married at the Community of the Holy Spirit's convent in New York City, where we'd met three years before, with our fabulous "Sound of Music wedding" being the first one orchestrated by the fourteen lovely nuns who

Madeleine with bride and groom, Sally and Mel Whitehead, February 1994.

lived there. Shortly before the service began, Madeleine arrived and joined me in my dressing room, where she joked with the sisters and gave me make-up tips from her theater days. ("Put your lipstick on, then tap your lips lightly with face powder. That way your lipstick will stay on though Mel's kiss," she laughed.)

The organ began to play, a sister motioned it was TIME, and we hurried to the chapel, Madeleine supported on one side by her cane and on the other by my arm. Stopping at the entrance, we quickly hugged before we began our procession down the chapel's short aisle. A moment before she presented me to Mel, Madeleine leaned into me heavily, so that for a moment, I was afraid she might be falling. Instead, she whispered words I'll never forget. "I feel just like I'm giving away my own daughter."

My heart soared as I kissed her again, thanked her for "everything" and told her she meant the world to me. Then I turned to face my smiling, soon-to-be husband. Cane in hand, Madeleine turned slowly, stood tall, and carefully made her way to her place by the sisters. Trying to focus on the upcoming vows, I couldn't forget how trite my words to Madeleine must have sounded and how they didn't come close to expressing the fullness of my heart. Glancing back at her once more, I only hoped she knew.

In just a few months, Mel and I made a difficult decision to move back to Georgia to reunite all the children and start a new life—one that has continued to grow and change as well it should. We returned to *our* New York City as often as possible. At first our visits included a happy reunion with Madeleine. Then, the day came when we were told by sad friends she was not well enough to receive company. It was okay, we consoled ourselves; surely we'd see her next time. Much to our sorrow, that proved untrue, and Mel and I never again saw our magnificent and lovely Madeleine again. And so life has come full circle: once more I turn to Madeleine's books to hear her voice.

> "Icons present an aspect of the Divine. They open doors for you to break away from human, chronological time; they put you into *Kairos* [which is] God's time. Stories are icons that open doors."
>
> —Madeleine L'Engle, Holy Cross Monastery, January 1991

How can I say goodbye to one so immeasurably dear? *(As I finish this simple homage, my full heart brims with love and appreciation for you, dear Madeleine.)* How can I conjure up so many treasured memories, my own extraordinary "wrinkles in time," and not have a container worthy and strong enough in which to hold them? This book, like my heart, is such a container. It is the purpose of all books—to contain what needs to be remembered. Madeleine's books were proof of that and so much more. For which I will forever remain her grateful student.

> "The message of a book must always be 'yes,' even if there is death, it still must be 'yes.'"
>
> —Madeleine L'Engle

The Chrysostom Society, Madeleine's beloved fellowship of Christian writers, Glen Eyrie Castle, Colorado Springs, 1997.

Madeleine's Gatherings

by Claudia Carlson

Claudia Carlson works as a graphic designer and illustrator. Her first book of poetry, The Elephant House, *was published by Marsh Hawk Press in 2007. She took Madeleine's CHS workshop in 1991.*

What made me a reader as a child? The usual. I was perpetually the new kid, and every September I made the same first impression: scrawny, nonstop running nose, and no skills in sports or age-appropriate chatter (I was the only child of an itinerant poetry professor who was also a single mom). I became fatalistic about the tyrannies of peers and teachers.

In third grade I came down with something that kept me out of school for three months, and into that golden hiatus came the worlds of books. First my mother read to me the *Chronicles of Narnia;* life was clearly better between the covers of our book club edition. I sailed on the *Dawn Treader,* I rode Aslan's back, and I was treated to fireside treats in Mr. Tumnus' curiously hobbit-like cave. Then I read *The Hobbit.* Better and better. At some point my reading sped up and I stopped moving my lips. My mother slipped in *Jane Eyre,* which featured a tortured orphan who liked to read in window seats, but the book grew boring; who cares about a grown-up becoming a governess to a dull girl? I devoured *The Wolves of Willoughby Chase* and reread the Narnia books. But, I was aware I didn't have a British accent, wasn't nearly as polite as these fictional children, and didn't live in the era of the Blitz or hoopskirts.

Then my mother gave me a copy of *A Wrinkle in Time.* This was magic of the best kind. Teenage misfits! In the here-and-now. Space travel. Science. Extraterrestrial adventures. And, like Lewis's books, a comfort that goes deeper than plot. I loved feisty Meg; she was real to me, and unlike Lucy, she wasn't born perfect.

I wasn't yet aware of Christian allegory. I'd been baptized at seven, leaving behind temple and Torah for church and choir. And even the Episcopalian phase of my upbringing was starting to wane by the time I came to L'Engle; my mom was already casting my horoscope and showing the signs of an incipient paradigm shift. I liked being in choir even though I didn't sing well; the choirmaster didn't mind, she only paused kindly when she could hear me and smiled the smile of turning the other ear. I sang very softly and felt the voices rise around me with awe.

It felt so good to be a part of something, in the austere and beautiful West Hartford choir loft, my fellow altos harmonizing around me. Even when my mother broke with the church, bought a bookshelf of astrology texts, and began to tell me just why Libras were given to procrastination, sarcasm, and messy bedrooms, I kept going, on my own, to whisper-sing. There was a memorable trip to New York City to the Cathedral of St. John the Divine, where we enjoyed its echo-distorting splendor. We were informed that the author of one of my favorite books was a writer in residence at this cathedral. But I didn't see her that day.

Then my mother made me a Unitarian; next we were embracing Zen, and zoom, we were back to Tarot and the stars and at some point I decided I was a N-O-T-H-I-N-G and planned to remain Switzerland to her Conquests in Meaning and Mysticism.

By college I was a secular humanist and majored in reading. I was now aware that Lewis and L'Engle had shaped their novels with Christian themes and were not afraid of allegory or its attendant spirit, language play. I read *Pilgrim's Progress* (ugh) and Spenser's *Fairy Queen* (had moments) and Swift (pure fun). I also took courses in Virginia Woolf, discovered Yeats, and eventually mastered essay writing. I even tried to embrace the idea that modern novels were not meant to be fun, that slogging through them gave me chops. Fellow majors told me I was bourgeois to want the affirming pablum of my childhood; they would jeer, waving their experimental nihilistic novels under my nose. And yet ... I missed those books. Books that fed more than my intellect. Books that had, in their one-sided way, befriended me.

I took to sneaking into the children's section of the university library. I'd borrow L'Engle and hide the books in plain brown paper wrappers so I wouldn't be caught by the novelistas roaming the lit halls in their caffeine-fueled tweed packs.

I was lucky enough to take a course on children's literature from a graduate student named Stephen Roxburgh. Here at last was affirmation that children's literature was worthy of study and respect. And had heart. Mrs Whatsit's description of life as a sonnet—we're given the form, but what we say is up to us—supplied a balm for something I hadn't been able to articulate as missing from my life.

I was rereading all the books I'd loved before I had the skills to dissect them. And despite my knowledge of themes and devices, subplots and metafiction, the books stood up. Roxburgh was an enthusiastic teacher just when I needed it. He went on to become a children's book editor at Farrar, Straus and Giroux, the publisher that first printed *A Wrinkle in Time.* He became Madeleine's editor.

A decade later I was living in the Upper West Side, near St. John the Divine, had two small children, and was working as a book designer; I worked at many publishing houses, including a year at Farrar, Straus and Giroux (where I never once saw L'Engle). A notice was brought to my attention about her writing workshop, offered through the Community of the Holy Spirit, a convent a few blocks away.

Should I take it? I wasn't religious, wasn't writing much, although I wanted to write, and how did I know if it would be any good? And what about those nuns?

The workshop was lovely. I found I enjoyed eating quietly with the nuns before we started working. Madeleine managed to distill a lifetime of writing and teaching into snappy advice and assignments. She exuded satisfaction and delight; her impish smile was both warm and knowing. There was no unkindness or backbiting. She understood that we urgently needed to express ourselves and doubted our ability to do it well. The calm spirit of the convent augmented the lively spirit of Madeleine. She asked us to not labor over the assignments and to write quickly to outfox our inner editors.

I wrote short stories about a fledgling witch who chose as her familiar a music box that played Bach and punk and that literally transported people. I started a romance set at a jumble sale. I rewrote family history to make a stolen ring return to its rightful owner. And finally, Madeleine asked us to write something in praise.

Writers crowd the living room of 924 West End Avenue, around 1995.

I went home stumped. I wasn't about to write about Jesus (as much as I admired his message of love and social justice). But I thought about what kept drawing me to the novels of people with strong faith. I craved narratives that were roadmaps to becoming a mensch. I loved the adventures of an evolving narrator as he or she navigated the way into adult life. Madeleine let us know she too had to learn and grow to become a person and writer; she wasn't born with these skills. Weren't these my hopes? I was glad I was a mother, and a writer despite not writing much, and I was grateful I was sharing this workshop with a compelling teacher and students who also yearned to express their muse, no matter its source.

I wrote in the spirit of the moment:

> "I thank the earth and air, fire and water that were used to make my children ... I praise the division of cells, the music of exponential mitosis, and the neural river flowing from their unawakened thoughts to the outreaching limbs. I praise the moment of feeling their first movement. I thank the voice that became their first cry. I thank most of all the miracle of their safe journey so that I could hold their perfect beginning near my heart."

I didn't know yet that I would become a poet, but the seeds were there.

I was never invited to become part of Madeleine's inner circle. There is something in me that resists even the best of gurus. But I loved Madeleine's yearly gathering of former students. Her magnificent apartment, with its views of my neighborhood and the Hudson River, soft upholstered seats, glowing colors and crisp patterns, was a visual meal. As we sat in a circle on her carpeted living room floor, Madeleine the center of our hub, I felt again much as I had in choir, each of us providing a harmony, as we told each other the cares and accomplishments that had shaped our year. We met with such a spirit of celebration that I was proud to be part of this group and came to understand my lack of religious faith was just a technicality. I belonged.

When I formed my own writing group, I drew upon the gently honest example of the workshop to improve craft while celebrating the creative spirit. We are now in our nineteenth year, and so it goes on. To gatherings.

Getting the Good News Across

by Genellen McGrath

Genellen McGrath is the director of the Gold Coast Public Library in Glen Head, New York, a library she helped to create. She is co-editor of the library newsletter. Genellen took Madeleine's CHS workshop in 1992.

"God never uses qualified people," she said, and instantly I felt comforted. Right away I knew this was not just another writers' workshop. Not that I'd expected it to be. This course wasn't held in an adult education classroom of a local high school, but at the Community of the Holy Spirit. The world-renowned Madeleine L'Engle was the teacher.

Having spent most of my life in and around books, the primary quality I brought to the table of aspiring writers that night was an appalling lack of credentials. Aside from having a childhood dream to write, I hadn't taken any formal writing classes either in high school or college. Not for lack of opportunity; the one teacher in my small women's college who did teach the topic gave me less than a lukewarm reception in her other English classes. So instead, I stuck with English literature as a major, and since I loved reading, it was a logical choice to pursue a master's degree in library science. Here I was, nearly ten years after college graduation, trying again.

"God isn't tidy," Madeleine explained, and although my thoughts ran to the piles of unfolded laundry, unmade beds, and dirty dishes I'd hastily left behind to make the hour-long trek from Oyster Bay, Long Island into Manhattan that evening, she conveyed to us the paradox of life in which pattern emerges from chaos, and our humanity lies in free will. I was admittedly all too human, having chosen to leave my two young children and husband every Tuesday evening for six weeks, while working part-time in my local library, to make this weekly pilgrimage in wintry darkness with two other women.

"Write a story," she commanded, "which never mentions Christ, but makes a Christian point. Make it true, but not factual." Who was this woman, who insisted that truth transcends and breaks through facts? I was a reference librarian, used to tracking down data through multiple sources, ensuring its constancy, before I was confident enough to comment on its veracity. I lived for the hunt, using nuggets of good information as if they were bread crumbs through a forest, leading to the one source that held the answer.

"Don't think when you write" sounded like outright heresy to me. After those baccalaurean days of laborious examination, analysis of character, and painstaking extraction of theme and plot, picking out the elements of symbolism, listing similes and metaphors; it seemed to me that works of fiction were sketched out first, on the warp threads of some great loom, weaving in the weft of prose, continuing with great care and planning as the tapestry unfolded. Almost mechanical, once the pattern was transcribed. How could thought not be involved? Practice, experiment, she said, don't worry about it being perfect. The highest form of prayer is beyond thought, when you are totally open to listen.

Writing was like prayer? This was not helpful. I wanted discrete tools and techniques, steps to follow so I could snare the filaments of inspiration that sometimes floated up into my conscious mind as I flipped through the pages of the newly published books at work. Prayer I was familiar with, but using that as a path to go beyond? I didn't know the way.

This sherpa of the written word confessed to learning *from* her stories, as she wrote what needed to be written and honored her characters. She told us that integrity and honesty had to be present for writing of quality. If we wrote out of our own pain and experience, it would work, as long as we wrote with our hearts as well as our heads. "Write out of need," she said.

So we started with that story, the one that made a Christian point without ever mentioning Christ. It is here that I have lost the facts, but remember the truth, since the bits and bytes of the original—and only—floppy disk version of that story are moldering away in a landfill somewhere by now. It was a story that sprang out of my need to know that I was in the right place that night, going in the right direction, for I had many doubts. I wanted confirmation that the things I wanted to say were of value and that I had some ability. Hope, I certainly had, but not faith.

I was not without fear in that room of strangers and Madeleine herself, despite her many references throughout that night to the Archangel Gabriel's greeting to the Virgin Mary: "Fear not!" After all, Madeleine said, Mary was getting good news. And so in my story I recounted the events that led up to my enrollment in this class. As with the miracle of Gideon's fleece in the Old Testament, dry when the ground was wet, and glistening with dew when the ground was dry, so too did I make a "deal" with God with respect to my presence in this writing class. Only I never mentioned God, just—like Gideon's fleece—my process of confirming that I belonged in the class. When I finished reading my piece aloud to the class that next week, I looked up at Madeleine, who smiled and nodded. I was on my way.

As the weeks progressed, I learned to open my heart, and my mind, to the characters and stories within. When I was able to grab some time for writing, I would sit quietly, wait, and listen. Whatever lay there, just outside my conscious reach, would meander into thought and take form on the page. It was terrifying at times, but thrilling. I was giving form to a hidden part of my character, an unfulfilled dream, my need to learn to write.

And I needed to be *there*, gathered around that table with other seekers, including mothers like myself, some fine artists, some people from the business world, some who were already writers, and one who was there simply because a pamphlet advertising this writing course swirled about the windy city street to stubbornly stick to her face. We were drawn to this woman, this humble, accomplished, and contemplative soul, who reassured us that our writing was neither a guilty pleasure nor a waste of time, but a transcendent experience, beyond control of the intellect.

Each week, we entered that realm, comforted by the routine of a simple repast before our lesson, and Compline afterwards, an evening prayer service at the convent that Madeleine explained was designed to send you to sleep. Our minds were opened, to ourselves and to each other, stretching the boundaries of our thought and plumbing the depths for new truths. In this safe place, varying stories and characters were incarnated under her caring tutelage. We became bigger, braver, and more real. We celebrated language, and when our facts failed to reveal those truths we had to tell, we reached out to faith to find them. In turn, she celebrated us, confirming our responsibility to the truth ... our responsibility to truly *listen.*

In the end, as I listened to Madeleine describe her early life in the theater, her marriage, family, and writing career, I learned that it didn't matter that my writing would be done in fits and starts. Writing is a process, like our lives, and we learn to grow in it. I learned I didn't have to be either a commercial or literary success as evidenced by the volumes surrounding me at my desk in the library. If I wrote what I understood, what I heard in that place beyond thought, chances were that it would resonate with others. I could both understand, and be understood. I could make connections between myself and others, be both the listener and the teacher. As if she knew this was bound to happen, Madeleine announced after the six-week class was over that participants in the workshop were invited once a year to her home.

And so I went, with my two nocturnal travelers, to the tradition that reunited scores of Madeleine's former students in her elegant apartment, every surface laden with a variety of culinary creations brought from tiny city kitchens or the depths of suburbia to nourish the body in anticipation of the celebration of authorship and artistry of all types. Those were evenings when character, time, and place all came together, as we shared the stories of our lives and listened to the stories we had written. As Madeleine once said, "We're all homesick for a home we don't know."

It has been seventeen years since I took that workshop, and I will cheerfully admit to being homesick for a time and place I did know, many years ago, where I sat in her presence and read aloud my first essay. So much has happened in the world since then; events have since transpired that shook Manhattan and the world. The church I knew was shaken by scandal, and my own career has undergone several changes as well. I hardly know that I work in a library anymore, surrounded by spreadsheets, insurance policies and invoices—the detritus of administration. For all I know, I am in the business of selling laundry soap, or manufacturing mattress coils; I am far removed from the beloved comfort of the library's book collection.

I write policies, procedures, and memos now; bimonthly I edit our newsletter. I am no longer surprised at the catchy phrases that just pop into my mind as I work with another librarian to craft a document that will interest and inform our community. After all, I am still connecting with these people, giving them good news about the programs and services of the public library they voted into existence just a few years ago. Over the past four years I have heard countless stories from these people, all with the same message: libraries are places of inspiration and hope. People have faith in them.

It's hope and faith I carry with me, confident that I made the right choices in my life; I may not be a professional writer, but writing is an important part of what I do. I have the belief that there is a time to everything. I no longer need Gideon's Old Testament fleece to know that writing is in my future. Instead I thank the New Testament's gifts of the Holy Spirit, the only qualification I need.

And I thank you, Madeleine.

Madeleine at 924 West End Avenue.

An Unexpected Gift

by Evelyn Rein

Evelyn Rein has published travel articles and is currently working on a book of short stories. She is also a printmaker. Evelyn took Madeleine's CHS workshop in the mid-1990s.

When I registered for Madeleine L'Engle's writing workshop in the 1990s I knew little about her. The only book I had read by her was *A Wrinkle In Time*, and although I found her to be an engaging writer the pervasive scriptural references in the book left me cold.

Having grown up in Alabama, where parents, schools, and communities used the Bible to enforce their own narrow and severely punitive rules, I had long ago closed the gate on religion. But since I was having difficulty writing, and since several writers had highly recommended Madeleine, I found myself one chilly autumn evening standing in front of St. Hilda's House on West 113th Street in New York City, where an Episcopal monastic order for women resided. I rang the bell.

A sister in a softly draped habit opened the door, her grey-white hair bobbing precariously over her forehead and friendly light blue eyes. She was not what I expected. As a child, I had been mystified and somewhat frightened of neighborhood nuns who called attention to themselves by disappearing beneath stiff, head-to-toe black "tents." This sister chatted easily about the weather and even seemed a little scattered; there was nothing at all formidable about her. She pointed upstairs where workshop members had assembled.

Twenty women sat around the long table, including several who had already taken the workshop at least once. Suddenly, all talking ceased. The door opened and Madeleine L'Engle swept in. Close to six feet tall, she was an erect stalk, yet she swayed, was fluid. Her feet were large, no-nonsense feet, yet seemed vulnerable, reminding me of a child in an awkward stage. Around her neck she wore a large, beaded multi-colored African necklace, a dramatic coup against the simple, straight purple dress that drifted softly to her ankles.

After introductions, Madeleine served a heady cocktail of great writers she had called on in her writing career: Shakespeare, Milton, Dante, Euripides,

Sophocles, Aristotle, Cervantes, Goethe, and Pascal. Einstein and relativity had, she said, fueled her imagination along with astrophysics and quantum mechanics. These writers were clearly part of her literary family, sources of inspiration, old friends.

When a short, petite dark-haired woman asked her if one of her books had been based on Paul, I learned Madeleine had yet another family, a Biblical one. This family was different. She spoke of Biblical figures in the same way she might have spoken of an uncle, a cousin, a sister. For example, she would say "I didn't like the way Mark spoke to ... " She held these characters' (characters to me, family to her) feet to the fire when she felt they acted irresponsibly or selfishly. Unlike my family's blind, unquestioning reverence for holy figures, when Madeleine spoke about Esther, Ruth, Matthew, or John, it was with the folksy, warm familial air prevalent at the large family reunions I had enjoyed so much as a child. Fascinated, I forgot to be offended (or threatened) that religion had found its way into our writing workshop.

Our assignment that first evening was to select any type of music and write a short story as we listened to it, which we would read the following week in class. I selected Schubert's *Trout Quintet,* and as I began to write, my mother's voice took hold. Her voice overrode my own inner voice as she told of her severe childhood hardships and the wounds left by my father, whom she had divorced—a familiar litany. Frustrated, I arrived the next week with no story in hand.

I headed downstairs, where large black pots were on the stove and a homey smell permeated the air. Workshop members had been invited to join the sisters each week for dinner. We sat at rectangular wooden tables that night and ate a hearty fish stew, crisp salad, and mixed-fruit pie. Madeleine, prompted by questions, spoke of the time when she was an actor, her marriage to the actor Hugh Franklin, and how they had left the stage and New York City to revive and run a defunct general store and raise a family in rural Connecticut. Happy when they returned to New York, she taught school and continued to write. In the bits and pieces of telling about ourselves, I recognized in Madeleine some of myself: our childhood awkwardness, not fitting in to the "norm." Emily Dickinson once said, "A wounded deer leaps the highest." What drew me to Madeleine was not her scars, but her determined leaps.

It was at these meals that I also took a shine to Sister Catherine Grace. She spoke of having been previously married, and through her I learned how like a family the order was, each sister having specific duties and all faced with the difficult challenges of living together, like all families. Sister Catherine Grace took her work seriously but at the end of the day often laughed infectiously as she confessed her strong liking for chocolate chip cookies. It was a revelation to recognize how alike we were.

After dinner I explained to Madeleine that I had been unable to complete my assignment because my mother had taken over the writing, a recurrent problem. "Let her," said Madeleine. *"Let her?"* What kind of advice was that? Hadn't I had it hammered into me by other writing teachers that we must find a way to dismiss unwanted voices? I took her advice. When I next wrote, I gave my mother free reign to say whatever she liked. Fighting the impulse to stop her had been exhausting, and it was a relief to give in. Strangely, when I allowed her to be the voice, she had very little to say. I realized I had such guilt about not listening to my mother's tales of woes and past hardships that, when I wrote, my guilt allowed her to take over. In allowing my mother to speak, I liberated my own voice as well.

Madeleine and Mother Madeleine Mary, CHS, 1990s.

The next week when workshop members sat down to dine with the sisters, total silence was observed. At first I felt awkward, but I learned how camaraderie can exist in silence, was aware of the bounty before us, and experienced a peacefulness that I usually kept at bay by being thoroughly preoccupied with my two daughters and husband.

After six short sessions, the workshop came to a close. Madeleine's faith did not become my faith—I'm still cobbling together my own spiritual path—but I did incorporate the tolerance she practiced and taught, a tolerance that cannot exist without listening to what others have to say. I still struggle, not with the concept, but with the commitment to listening. Then I am reminded of Madeleine's injunction to be patient but at the same time echoing Churchill's words, to "Never, never, never, never give up."

What I remember most about Madeleine was her boldness. She dared to be unorthodox in her thinking and in her advice to writers. She dared to be a Christian liberal, not a literalist, often invoking the ire of religious conservatives. And she had dared to persevere: over six million copies of the many times rejected *A Wrinkle in Time* have been sold, and she went on to publish some sixty books. Most of all, though, she dared not to let the public's response, whether backlash or adulation, divert her from writing, from pursuing her search for truth.

In *A Wrinkle In Time,* Mrs Who's gift to Meg, the protagonist, was a pair of glasses through which she could see dark evil in the world and therefore defend against it. Madeleine's gift to me was a pair of glasses that revealed not dark evil, but a welcome ray of light.

924 West End Avenue.

Writers' workshop around the oval table, St. Hilda's House, 1989.

The Storyteller, the Icon, and Me

by Patricia McMahon Barry

Patricia McMahon Barry is a poet and an attorney who attended Madeleine's writing workshop at Holy Cross Monastery in 1993. On Pat's wedding day in 1998, Madeleine helped give her away and was her "mentor of honor."

"Listen to the story." This is how Madeleine L'Engle started her writing workshop at Holy Cross Monastery in West Park, New York in January 1993. I had listened intently to her story, *A Wrinkle in Time*, read aloud by my third-grade teacher, Sister Josephine, in Hartford, Connecticut some thirty years before that night. Now, on a winter's night far removed, the author herself was telling me to listen to something new: my own, yet unwritten, story.

In the early 1990s I had read two of Madeleine's later works, *Walking on Water: Reflections on Faith and Art* and *Two-Part Invention: The Story of a Marriage;* I found that Madeleine addressed the subjects of writing and love in a forthright way that was both concrete and spiritual. I had had a talent for writing in school and felt drawn to the idea Madeleine expressed that we act in the image of the loving Creator when we write. And I had no boyfriend at the time and wanted to hear this wise woman speak about love. And so I came to Holy Cross for both Madeleine's writing workshop and her silent retreat—to listen, learn, write, and pray. The experience would prove to be a highlight of my life.

I listened. Madeleine told us that writing is an act of letting go, listening, and remembering: writing in a way that's listening, not controlling. You don't turn off the intellect, just its control. "Remembering, when you're ready" was an act of heart and mind together, remembering in Plato's sense that all learning is remembering. You must be child-hearted, have that willingness to "re-member" which is not about memory so much as about "putting back together," she said, "like the Body and Blood of Christ."

This last thought shocked me: I hadn't thought of those elements as ever separated. But this first night was about new ideas that would become clearer later. I was grateful that Madeleine closed the session by saying that we all think too much, and our assignment for that night was to re-member something: we were to quiet our mind, listen for a while, five to fifteen minutes, and at the end of that time write, just write. "Something will demand to be written," she said with complete confidence. "Write it—a short story—for no more than one hour, including re-membering. Then go to sleep."

I was no stranger to quieting my mind, a step in the silent prayer called Centering that I had been practicing with a group at my home parish in Queens for some three years. In our darkened church, we aimed to gently silence the mind and so become aware of God inside us. Madeleine's instruction that night, "Be patient, listen. Be patient with silence; it will speak," sounded right. With God in the silent darkness, I felt I would find story there too.

My story that night began with the green color of the blotter on my writing table, led back to green chairs in my childhood kitchen, similar chairs in someone else's kitchen years later, a dining room scene that concluded with my recent breakup after a long relationship, and a green light at the crossroads I saw before me then. It was a winding path I followed as I let it unfold, tell itself to me, as I put pen to paper that night. Madeleine would later say that there was a lot in that story.

Madeleine said, "We do not stay in the same place when we write; we don't control it. It's about losing control. We move from where we are to where God takes us." I realized this had happened in my short story.

Remembering, Loving, and Writing

In the silent retreat, Madeleine returned to the theme of the Body and Blood of Christ. "We know the Incarnation every day in the breaking of the bread. We belong to each other and to God." In Communion, "We are graciously given God, partake of God, and offer God to each other." Madeleine's view of God's presence and our action at Mass brought to mind Jesus' words in the liturgy: "Do this in memory of me." I realized that what Madeleine had just described was indeed re-membering, as in putting back together. The image I thought of was of Jesus saying, "I am here, now. My body and blood are gathered and re-membered into each of you. My essence—my love for you—is present here and now and always."

"Christ was always available," Madeleine showed us during the silent retreat, in images from art about the Old Testament—a large raven feeding Elijah a communion host; King David holding a harp in one arm and the child Jesus in the other—and throughout history since then.

When Madeleine described an El Greco of St. Andrew and St. Francis, separated by hundreds of years, talking to each other with the crucifix between them, I found myself remembering that there had been a crucifix on the wall of every one of my classrooms at St. Peter's School, the alabaster Jesus nailed to the ebony cross. Returning to that memory at night, I felt Jesus' love had always been available for me too, though I didn't realize it or particularly feel it during those grade-school years as an awkward, shy child, tall and serious. My mother, who had died the year before I came to this workshop, was on my mind too. I began to realize that I had had all that I needed so long ago to go forward as a loved person into the present, to make the choices a loved person makes.

One such choice, for me, is to write. Writing risks intimacy with the reader and is both a vulnerable and courageous act, like love. I had shared my writing—usually poetry—only in classrooms or with professors, to mark special occasions. I didn't want to be judged and rejected by editors and publishers. Madeleine said in the writing workshop that you must be willing to be vulnerable, to listen to the work, to let it surprise you, to get courage from it, to risk, to learn by failure as no other creature does. It sounded exciting, and humbling. "Offer it with love," Madeleine said, "without too much pride. We have to reach out if God throws the ball." Madeleine called writing "a cosmic decision," affecting "everyone you know," and not so much a choice as an imperative: "We write because we have to, because it saves us and will save the universe."

It was freeing to hear her say that writing was God's gift, given in love and meant to be shared the same way. After all, what had enabled me to move beyond fears of being judged as a Eucharistic minister and then a lector had been realizing that the Mass was not, after all, about me, and would go forward whatever mistake I might make: stumbling over words, dropping the hosts, whatever. The miracle of Jesus' presence in the Eucharist would happen no matter what. Writing wasn't about me, either; putting writing in the context of sharing the gift God has given, and offering it with love, made sense. But I would have to write, sit down and write on a regular basis, to offer the gift. Madeleine called it "being obedient to the work"; I called it writing "faithfully." I began to feel motivated to write more and share more of my writing in that spirit.

For I see today more than ever that we are all connected. Although I had been shocked to think of the separation of Body and Blood on that first night of Madeleine's workshop, I was stunned to see that I had been deepening and regularly falling into a divide I hadn't realized existed, separating the not-really-separate elements of the gift, its source (God), its reason (love), its use (writing and sharing), and its effect (loving and helping others). I was writing hardly at all and keeping it to myself. Madeleine invited—no, called—me to understand something I vaguely knew to be true: the gift of writing is meant to be used and shared like life itself, with mind and heart together and for the good of all. My greater awareness of this truth would result in greater sharing of myself and my gift for writing. Keeping that gift to myself, failing to use and share it, didn't make sense any more.

Icons for Change

During the silent retreat, Madeleine said that an icon depicts or stands for an aspect of someone or something that we need, that is important to us. An icon won't let us stay in one place or be satisfied. "It thrusts us out an open door and gives a wider vision." "If we live life iconically, it's wide open, nothing is closed. God may say no but nobody else can." And "we are meant to be icons for each other" by being with the people we are with "wholly and fully," as Jesus was. Madeleine described Jesus as fully present to the people he encountered: He ate with them, told stories, healed them, loved and forgave them. "This intimacy is forbearing, not permissive: it gives courage to look at ourselves and believe we're able to do more, be more."

Madeleine spoke of her icons: dolphins for safety, as they would leap and dance in Florida waters where sharks were absent; penguins for the precious and fragile nature of intimacy where skewers are a daily threat to penguin eggs; Eva Le Gallienne for the way she approached her art of acting, "always ready to change something, to try another way that might work better." All of these icons spoke to me too.

I didn't expect that I would find an Annunciation icon at the Holy Cross gift shop. I was just looking for gifts for friends and something that might inspire me. The diptych I found (I later learned it was a tiny version of Fra Angelico's fresco, "The Annunciation") showed Mary dressed in light pink with a black mantle across her lap; the Archangel Gabriel bent opposite her imploringly, his colorful wings barely tucked behind him as he stepped into the garden room where she was seated, her arms crossed below her bosom mirroring his greeting. I was drawn to this image of Mary, and not just because my birthday is March 25, the usual date of the feast of the Annunciation; I felt it would help me change for the better, encourage me to walk more confidently into the garden of life. I brought it and another small diptych—showing Our Lady of Perpetual Help on one side and Christ the Lawgiver on the other—to the counter to buy them. When the shopkeeper monk told me with furrowed brow that he hadn't seen either diptych come in to the shop, I knew that they were meant for me.

At our last session of the retreat, I shared why these two diptychs, taken together, were an icon to me. The Annunciation scene showed Mary as a pale and vulnerable young woman in a room with grid-like bars on the window and a garden outside. The choice she was about to make would mean leaving that room and all it represented: her tradition, plan, and logic, even her idea of a God who did not have a son. A door was opened and her faith, body, mind, and heart were thrust through it. Her acceptance was key: Mary's "yes" spoke Christ into being.

The Perpetual Help/Lawgiver diptych was almost the polar opposite: a close-up family picture in rich, deep maroon and blue against a golden background, Byzantine icons well-matched. I described Mary's hands and arms tenderly holding the young Jesus, his sandal dangling from running to her after the ultimate bad dream of the crucifixion. Here was Mary giving comfort and aid to Jesus, her eyes looking at me with full knowledge of the cross to come. I had to look with a child's heart to see those elements of intimacy that had felt largely missing for me in my childhood. The diptychs made clear that the pale Virgin Mary of the Annunciation became the Mother of Perpetual Help, able to give comfort, aid, and love abundantly and with wisdom. I told the group that I took hope for myself from these scenes of transformation in giving love and getting wisdom.

When a fellow member of the retreat said that Mary did not leave her tradition as I had said, Madeleine was quick to reply that this was what I felt about Mary, and there was nothing wrong with that. I loved her saying this, and realized that Madeleine was no stranger to defending the integrity of imagination and the fruits of meditation against a too-literal approach to matters of the spirit.

I also shared with the group that Madeleine had taken me back to my childhood to realize that God and God's love had always been fully there for me, in Christ who was always available, and that this love was enough and would not be taken away.

The child I had been, the woman I was, and the person I would aim to become had come together at Madeleine's workshop and retreat; each had had a story to tell me, and I had listened.

"And experience worketh hope . . ."

In quoting that portion of Romans 5:4, Madeleine spoke of "the hope that we will know and understand that God loves us, and take that love and put it in our hearts to shine for the whole world to see." Throughout the workshop and retreat, Madeleine spoke with authority and from her own experience, sharing what she knew to be true about writers and the solitary nature of the act of writing, encouraging us to write, to have faith in God and ourselves and our gift, and to share it with others.

The logic, sense, and spirituality in all of this, as expressed by Madeleine, were undeniable. Her height and elegance befitted her artistry; the grace and beauty of her reasoning, even in conversation, reflected her writing voice. She dramatically held forth on the page and in person in tones lyrical or flat as it suited her purpose, speaking without notes about her art, other writers, music, the necessity to keep going on despite rejection, and the importance of sharing our work, even speaking it out loud.

Madeleine provided the shove I needed to begin writing regularly and more seriously, and her perspective gave me the courage and reason to share my poetry and essays. On the last day of the retreat, I started looking for a writing group. I had met Stephanie Cowell, who was then working on her Nicholas Cooke trilogy, during the first days of the workshop; like me, she had stayed on for the retreat. We shared a love of books in general and Shakespeare in particular. She told me that a writing group might be starting in the fall from Madeleine's next workshop.

In October I called Stephanie and she put me in touch with Sally Lowe (Whitehead) and children's book author and artist Sanna Stanley; they had just completed the latest workshop in New York City. And so our writing group was born. Sally soon married Mel Whitehead, left the group, and moved back to Georgia. Pam Leggett and Jane Gardner completed workshops and joined our group practically at the same times. Finally, Andrea Simon, whose books include *Bashert: A Granddaughter's Holocaust Quest,* came to us through a mutual friend. The group members—Sanna, Pam, Jane, Andrea, and I—have remained together through two weddings, mine and Sanna's; motherhood for Pam and Sanna; and Sanna's move to Connecticut and Jane's to North Carolina (Jane participates in our meetings by phone). I value their friendship, sharing, and encouragement more than I can begin to say.

In the years that followed my first workshop and retreat, I had the privilege of attending gatherings at Madeleine's home and driving Madeleine to or from some happy milestones: to Stephanie's wedding to Russell Clay and home from the christening of Pam's daughter, Krista. Madeleine's time was so closely scheduled (she used pencil only, frequently borrowed, on her calendar) and willing drivers so many that someone else would usually drive her back home from where I drove her and vice-versa. But our attention to each other ran both ways: she was fully present to me and I to her as we discussed poetry and opera, my direction in life and her travels.

It was an honor for me to share that drive-time with her and to attend workshop-alumni gatherings at her apartment: as she presided over those gatherings in her armchair, the other guests and I would encircle her with food, stories, and our love. I would write a poem for those times and read it aloud there. Madeleine's openness, courage, and welcoming spirit were evident in the simply incredible act of inviting this large group into her home. I on the other hand had

Patricia Barry, Andrea Simon, Sanna Stanley (with son, Bennett Sprague), and Pamela Leggett, January 2005.

Patricia McMahon Barry and Madeleine, August 1998.

closed-in, but gradually expanding, ways and a cluttered apartment. Madeleine inspired me. What she had said in that silent retreat, "We are meant to be icons for each other," was true of the way she lived her life: fully present to others. Madeleine was present to me in a way that gave me courage to look at myself and believe I was able to do more and be more.

Around the same time, I took one more writing workshop with Madeleine, at the Community of the Holy Spirit convent in New York; it was there that she took one of her favorite quotes—Canon West's statement about creating, "It is the nature of love to create; God is love and God creates"—one step further. In answer to a question about life after death, Madeleine said, "The loving consciousness that created us would never abandon us." These truths built upon each other and spoke to my heart.

When I married Robert in 1998, Madeleine came to my wedding and helped give me away. Both of my parents were dead and Madeleine was my "mentor of honor." Her presence reminded me of the transformation I had believed possible on a winter's retreat in 1993; we celebrated with joy and hope on that sun-filled August day.

On one of our vacations in Greenville, New York, Robert was driving us back to our resort from a restaurant; the country road was twisty, the night was pitch black, and we could barely see. I prayed, and what came to mind was Madeleine's statement that the loving consciousness that created us would not abandon us. Robert and I stayed calm, talked each other through the way back, and arrived safely. I returned home to e-mails from my writing group about Madeleine's death that week. I stopped cold at my computer, stunned. Although I had not seen her in some years, Madeleine had helped me in a real way that night in Greenville around the time of her death. "There are no coincidences," Madeleine had quoted someone else as saying, "only miracles in which God chooses to remain anonymous." Madeleine was with God now, part of that loving consciousness. I felt her loss deeply and shared the Greenville story with my writing group that day. In the weeks that followed, I began to write more, feeling some urgency and that time was short. I was keenly aware of the difference one writer's life can make in the lives of many. And I knew that Madeleine's devotion to writing, along with her friendship and her faith, had changed me for the better.

Our writing group, which had been meeting infrequently at that time, pledged to continue meeting, in memory of Madeleine. Pam took notes in pencil and sent out an e-mail confirming that we'd meet quarterly, have a quorum rule, and rotate our meeting place among our homes.

Madeleine told me toward the end of my first retreat with her, "Don't deny your own gifts." I "hold down" that statement, as she would say, and am going forward using and sharing my gifts, in the spirit God intended as far as I can discern it. I have Madeleine's powerful perspective on this, and her invaluable example and that of my writing group, to guide me.

Here are some of my favorite quotes from Madeleine's workshops and retreat:

- Be aware each day that the universe and eternity is ahead of you; something new can happen, good or bad.
- God made *us* all. What every one of us does affects the cosmos. Every risk we take with love and hope makes a difference, brings the coming of the kingdom a little closer.
- So you must put the writing first—shut out everything you're not responsible for—no one will love you for it. You please God and yourself when you write—nobody else. But come back happy about what you've written.
- A lot of writing is in the realm of unknowing, like praying. If you write while you're listening, the best things are not yours; they're "other." We're vehicles—it's not ours. Be a good vehicle, a good instrument: then let go and let it be played.

Meeting Madeleine

by Terryl Wiley Anderson

Terryl Wiley Anderson is a former professional ballet dancer and ballet teacher. She left the arts to enter the business world in sales. Discovering a desire to write, Terryl returned to the arts and theater by writing and directing plays and skits; she has recently begun work on her first novel. Terryl took Madeleine's workshops at CHS beginning in 1994.

It is October 1994, a Tuesday evening, and I am in a very unlikely place. I am walking up the dim, dark grey, concrete steps of a convent in New York City. I ring the bell. After a minute the door is opened by a little grey-haired nun who smiles sweetly. The inside entryway is bright and warm. I hear laughter coming from another room. She ushers me to a tiny elevator, pushes the button for me, and closes the door. The elevator bumps and rattles to the upper floor. I open the door cautiously. The hallway is very quiet, my footsteps embarrassingly loud. I find the conference room; it is narrow and empty except for a long table and chairs.

As I wait I marvel at how fortunate I am, a Minnesotan transplanted to New Jersey, to be in this place and about to meet *the* Madeleine L'Engle. I heard about Madeleine's workshops from friends who attended last year, and I made certain I was one of the first to register. Now I wonder about the other women of various ages who arrive. Are they writers? Have they been published? Are any like myself, a newcomer to writing?

As participants fill the chairs, more chairs are added and these too fill. Then Madeleine arrives. She enters, tall and regal, and immediately fills the room with her presence. She walks the length of the room to sit at the head of the table. More women and one man arrive and, though I know the class has a limited enrollment, Madeleine invites them to join us. She asks us all to squish together to make room for them, and we are happy to do it. (I will later learn this kind of thing happens at her own dining table.) In a way it is dining that we have come to do. Dine at Madeleine's feet from her wisdom, her discipline, and her experiences with writing. The writing exercises we will do are not half as interesting to me as feasting on her words and her hospitality.

She adjusts her chair, places her folded hands resolutely on the table, and looks around at each of us. We each share a little bit of our lives and why we have come. She turns in her chair to face each person, listening. I see that she is both a commanding leader and a kind mother to us. Our version of the Queen Mum.

As others talk, I focus on Madeleine. She is wearing a long-sleeved grey-blue dress with a pretty design stitched on the V-neck and bodice. She has drop earrings, a long, heavy necklace, and a knobby bracelet, which are just right for her large frame. Her jewelry speaks of her love of the arts. I envision her buying jewelry at a New York City art fair. She is bold, but elegant and comfortable with herself. I do not like her short hairstyle, yet as I try to visualize different lengths and styles on her, I have to cover up a smile. I decide that for her, short hair is perfect.

Over the next six Tuesdays, we would learn a lot about writing and more about Madeleine. It was obvious that she loved her flock of writers and she loved this venue for teaching. Madeleine was Madeleine with us. She shared her likes and dislikes; she shared injustices that made her angry and allowed us to see her vulnerable side. Madeleine was a faithful follower of Jesus. All she said and did revealed her beliefs and her strong faith.

At our first session she talked about story and its importance in our lives. She emphasized showing, not telling, the story. She encouraged us to be true to the spirit and characters of our story. For Madeleine the spirit was The Spirit, God's Holy Spirit.

Madeleine also loved poetry. She spoke of the Bible as being rich in both stories and poetry. She read the Bible every day. She read it like a book, from cover to cover, and then started over again. And she devoured the psalms, reading at least two psalms morning and evening. One of our assignments was to rewrite one of the psalms in our own words. I found this to be one of the hardest assignments, but there were those in class who wrote some beautiful present-day psalms. Whenever someone read a poem or a psalm Madeleine asked that it be read a second time. "I have to hear it at least twice," she would say. Then she would sit up taller, close her eyes, take a breath in and out, and drink the words into her being.

I learned a lot about how to just "be" from Madeleine, especially from her book *A Circle of Quiet*. She told how she would often go to her star-gazing rock, where she would put her feet into the cold mountain water or climb onto the rock, gaze at the stars, and simply "be." "After all," she would say, "we are human b-e-i-n-g-s."

Madeleine's directions for assignments were always the same. "Take as much time to think as you would like, then write for half an hour, and when you write—don't edit!" (This technique was extremely freeing for me, and I still use it today.)

When we read our pieces each week it was obvious that Madeleine loved hearing our different writing voices, and she spoke encouraging words to each of us. She never complimented the work just to be nice, but found small or large gems in our work to praise. Madeleine applauded writing that moved her to smile or laugh and writing that spoke directly to her heart. As much as she liked words, Madeleine thought the English language frequently inadequate. An example she used was the word *love*. Other languages have several words for *love*. We *love* ice cream, our families, sports, and our country with the same little word.

Madeleine enjoyed words but she disliked labels. She certainly did not like it when she was labeled a Christian writer or a writer of children's books. She was a writer. She was a Christian. It was ridiculous, she thought, to be introduced as a children's writer because she never wrote specifically for children. She told us that good writing is good, bad writing bad—for everyone. She taught that children deserved the *best* writing, and children recognized good writing even if they could not tell why. (This has inspired me to write my best and never settle for mediocre work.)

Madeleine reminded us that language evolves and changes with time. She revealed her hurt that *Wrinkle* had been blacklisted by a segment of the Christian community. She told us it was because of a couple of words, and these words

Madeleine and Terryl Anderson.

had different meanings now than when *Wrinkle* was written. She was deeply wounded that some of her fellow Christians could be so judgmental.

Another of Madeleine's assignments was to write a *good* mom story. She said she had a very good mother and she was tired of bad mother stories. I will always remember that she liked a line from my story, "Mom was in the kitchen rattling pans—all was right with the world." Madeleine smiled at me and her eyes held mine. I felt deeply loved.

Once Madeleine shared with us that she was more than halfway through a book she was writing when suddenly a character showed up and insisted on being in her book. She told this character emphatically that he did not belong in this book, but the character was equally emphatic and demanded that he be put in. This discourse went on for a while. In the end Madeleine agreed, even though it meant a lot of rewriting to work him into the book from the beginning. This character was Joshua in *The Arm of the Starfish.* I have since learned firsthand what she was talking about. I was writing a story when suddenly it started going in a whole new direction. I decided to follow the course the story wanted to take. The new ending was more powerful and tapped into a much deeper meaning than I ever could have imagined. Madeleine taught me that the work often knows best. Her truths and teachings are still fresh and alive years later.

I was also fortunate to attend two of the writers' reunions that took place in Madeleine's New York apartment. Everyone brought a favorite dish of food to share. We nodded at the doorman in the lobby, he nodded back; he knew exactly where we were going. We rode another bumpy, bangy elevator to her floor, and we all smiled.

Like Madeleine, the apartment was elegant. The high-ceilinged rooms were stately and beautiful. I can still see the carved moldings, the grand piano, the oil paintings, and the subtle colors in the oriental carpet. But most of all I remember the long row of windows that faced west, with their view of the Hudson River and the rose-colored sunset beyond.

The halls were filled with shelves, ceiling to floor. The shelves were filled with books! Ironically, I did not find one of her own books until I wandered into the rooms behind the kitchen, which long ago had been servants' quarters. There metal shelves held copies of the various printings of her books. I would not dare to enter her beautiful bedroom, but I did glimpse small piles of books she was reading by the bed and the chair. In fact, there were small stacks of books everywhere: the bathroom, the end tables, even the entryway where she took off her boots.

Madeleine sat in her winged chair and welcomed each guest. From this chair she ruled her home with Southern hospitality, grace, and charm. After dinner there was time to share what people were working on. There were publishing announcements, and life changes—a marriage! A new baby! Madeleine was always thrilled to learn that small writers' groups had formed out of the workshops. Some groups that had formed several years earlier were still meeting and new groups were starting. My small group still gets together, and she encouraged us at her reunions to keep meeting. It was wonderful! I enjoyed every part of those gatherings—yet all I wanted to do was sit in the attractive green sofa next to that winged chair and drink in Madeleine herself.

Madeleine in Chicago, 1998.

Room to Grow

by Claire Joy, CHS

Claire Joy, CHS, is a member of the Community of the Holy Spirit in New York City. Before her call to the religious life she was an artist for thirty years, working in photography, television and AV production, 3-D animation, and graphic design. She has exhibited on the Episcopal Church and Visual Arts (ECVA) website. Claire Joy enjoys creating cartoons and writing a blog called "Flavor of the Month." She took Madeleine's CHS workshop in the mid-1990s.

I remember when I first started coming to the convent for Madeleine's writing workshops. At the time I was working as a graphic designer for *Stagebill* magazine, and a friend at church happened to mention the workshop in passing. I must admit my interest was more in meeting the famous Madeleine L'Engle than in developing my writing skills.

That was to change, and quickly. I had written a little poetry and some short stories, but I was already a somewhat talented visual artist. It didn't seem right to start claiming to be a writer too. Madeleine changed my mind with her frank critiques and encouraging comments. She believed in creativity and the creative process, not in false modesty.

I wound up taking Madeleine's workshop for three successive years, and would have continued, had she continued offering them, but a necessary hip operation ended our final class a few weeks early. She was not well enough to offer them again.

I remember my first year: I'd been on a waiting list for months, and was fortunate to get a spot. The evening of the first class I arrived at the convent before 5:30 and rang the doorbell. I waited . . . and waited . . . and waited. From somewhere deep inside the bowels of the cloister a disembodied voice answered, "Yes?"

"I'm here for Madeleine's workshop."

"I'll be right there."

Eventually a sister dressed in black came to the door and ushered me up the two flights of stairs to the chapel. Her skirts swished as we ascended the staircase, no talking, all very hush-hush. The place was *so quiet*, but the stairs wouldn't cooperate.

They creaked. I found myself trying to climb and tiptoe at the same time.

I came early, so there was time to meditate and pray briefly. The pews creaked too. Shhhh! I thought to myself as I tried to maneuver from seat to kneeler and back again.

Then Vespers began and I was awash in the medieval chant of the psalms. Those of us who were visiting tried to sing along, but the tones and the endings kept changing, and the guests didn't have pointed music, only the prayer book. Some of the women (who thought they knew the music) bellowed it out and their mistakes were obvious. There was a welcome card at each seat that instructed us to *sing softly*. Not everyone paid attention to that. *I* sang softly (and felt pretty smug about it). Smugness is hardly a monastic virtue, however, and five years later, when I *was* one of the sisters myself, I *had* the music to refer to. I came to appreciate how much courage it took to risk getting it wrong.

St. Hilda's House, the Community of the Holy Spirit's Manhattan residence.

Madeleine's class did not set me on my journey to the convent, but it introduced me to the space, the quiet, and to the sisters themselves. Through that association I was offered an art exhibition in the convent's art/piano room. Madeleine was kind enough to endorse the event in class, and several writers attended.

As they say, the rest is history. I entered the convent in July 2003 and was received as a postulant in October. I made my life profession in December 2007. Four years of candidacy... a series of gradual and painful conversions. I learned that comparison is an illusion created by something *other* than God. *We* are unique. Getting things *wrong* actually seems to be part of God's plan. I wish I'd known that sooner.

Madeleine seemed to know it instinctively. She gave us plenty of room to get it wrong. Her comments and critiques of our writing endeavors were always positive and humorous. I loved the assignments she gave and the practical advice about writing. "Think about the topic as long as you like," she said. "But once you sit down to write, don't stop. Don't edit. Just write for half an hour." I find that today, even when I blog, I stick to her advice: half an hour, non-stop, edit later.

My favorite assignment (which she repeated for more than one class) was to pick a character from the Bible, one we *didn't* like, and tell the story from that person's point of view. My first attempt was with Cain. I wrote it as a humorous piece, describing his mother's first experience with childbirth without drugs, of Adam's subsequent guilt-turned-on-Cain for all her screaming. Everyone laughed.

The next time Madeleine assigned that topic, I tackled Satan. It was my first attempt at a serious piece of theological interpretation, and not especially successful. I had much more luck when I took a humorous approach. That one assignment planted a seed, though. It has sprouted in an unusual way, in that I now draw cartoons—about God ... and Satan ... and nuns ... all the standard clichés. Humor takes the edge off and allows me to suggest things that wouldn't fly any other way. I was able to develop the beginnings of that style in Madeleine's workshops. Her wisdom and encouragement were both teaching and example. She is alive in all the lives she touched, and I am forever grateful that she touched mine.

Madeleine, Victoria, and Me

by Claire Whitcomb

Claire Whitcomb, the former editor-at-large of Victoria *magazine, is a brand writer at Eileen Fisher. She has written five decorating and history books, including* Real Life at the White House, *co-authored with her father, John Whitcomb.*

I met Madeleine L'Engle over tea at the St. Regis Hotel in New York in the summer of 1994. I was with Nancy Lindemeyer, the editor of *Victoria*, who wanted to hire Madeleine as writer in residence. Nancy loved *Summer of the Great-Grandmother* and believed in women who didn't look like their book jacket pictures—Madeleine took us aback initially because she was a decade or two older than the woman in her author's photo. Over the next year, I worked as Madeleine's editor, overseeing the pieces she wrote for the magazine. I stayed in her circle as a regular at her writing workshops. We lived two blocks from each other on West End Avenue, sharing the apartment number 95, and once I got her mail. Madeleine remains a powerful force in my life. She unlocked the key to fiction and modeled a way of living deeply and creatively in community. Here is an adaptation of the profile I wrote for *Victoria*. It launched her writer-in-residency in January 1995.

What lingered after you met Madeleine L'Engle was her voice, an exuberance of words that tumbled toward a decisive finale. "I started writing when I was five," she said. "It never *occurred* to me that it was something you were supposed to worry about." Then came a pause. "You learn to write by *doing* it." Her delivery, crisp and no-nonsense, reminded you that she spent her early years as a stage actress; her sense of timing was superb.

On the afternoon of my visit, much was askew. The kitchen at Crosswicks, her Goshen, Connecticut home, was being redone for the first time since she was pregnant with her son, Bion, some 40 years ago. No one had even the faintest idea where a vase for flowers might be. Madeleine's ankle was giving her trouble, and the dogs leapt in three directions when she got their leashes, nearly knocking her over. Rain clouds hovered over the Litchfield Hills. But when she smiled and gestured with her long-fingered hands, the hands of a piano player, all seemed right with the world.

The centerpiece of a very extended family, Madeleine was orbited by three children, assorted grandchildren, and nineteen godchildren. *Nineteen*? "Some of them I acquired at birth, others have come to me along the way," explained Madeleine. Was there an application process? She laughed as she talked about one young man she'd been considering taking on for some years—I don't know if she ever did. "I take being a godparent very seriously," she explained. "I am *in* their lives."

At Crosswicks, the living room showcased a lampshade she covered with now-peeling children's book covers, including, front and center, *Madeline*. Rubber bands were kept on a wooden giraffe—she thought of herself as a giraffe because of her long neck and a gangly gait that caused her to be last picked for the hockey team. In her study over the garage, a former chicken coop nicknamed the Ivory Tower, Madeleine wrote at her father's desk. For many years she used his portable typewriter, given to her when she was in fifth grade, until the *e* began to stick, requiring her to pull it down with a wrench. "After my fourth book, my agent said to my husband, Hugh, 'Can't you buy Madeleine a new typewriter?'"

The new typewriter acquired another use. When people asked her, "How did you manage to write when you were having children?" she answered, "With great conflict, with great frustration." She often fell asleep on top of her typewriter.

Questions about life—"Why am I here; who am I; do our individual lives matter"—demanded exploring. "Those are nice big questions that people who are grown-up think they shouldn't ask anymore," she said. "I think we should. One reason I make many of my protagonists young adolescents is that is the age at which the questions are most openly being asked."

In her own life, Madeleine has not always had the answers. For two and a half years, *A Wrinkle in Time* was turned down by publisher after publisher. "This book was my heart's belief, my psalm of praise. I was not prepared for the rejection. But I had a female protagonist; the word 'tesseract' was not on any vocabulary list; editors said children were not prepared for a book about evil. 'Who is this written for?' they'd ask. I'd put the kids to bed and take the dogs and walk down the dirt road in front of our house and bellow at God: 'I wrote this for you.'"

Her last rejection of *A Wrinkle in Time* occurred on a Monday before Christmas. She wrapped presents, not realizing she'd designated a necktie for a three-year-old and perfume for a man. Madeleine's mother, who happened to be visiting, suggested the book be sent out once more, to a friend who worked at the publisher Farrar, Straus and Giroux. "He gave it to a librarian to critique," recalled Madeleine. "She didn't like it, saying it reminded her of *The Wizard of Oz.*" Fortunately, the editor disagreed. He took Madeleine out to lunch and told her, "We love this book, but we want you to know no one is going to buy it."

With its fifty-third hardcover printing, *A Wrinkle in Time* was keeping Madeleine's mailbox full. She received about a hundred letters a week and answered them all, some with a carefully composed form letter about the latest happenings in her life. But questions of faith, stories about a reader's marriage and those nice big questions about life received personal responses.

Madeleine divided her time between Connecticut, New York, and the rest of the world. She taught writers' workshops at major institutions (the University of New Mexico, for instance) as well as the Community of The Holy Spirit in New York City. She preached at the Congregational Church in Goshen and led Lenten Meditations at the Cathedral of St. John the Divine, where she began a thirty-odd year stint as a church librarian when the regular librarian went on jury duty and never came back.

She played piano, took dogs for walks on country roads, sat out by the brook at Crosswicks, kept journals, and believed in paying attention to what she called "the underneath part, the part that comes up when I'm writing."

Always she argued with God, finding that as she aged, life persisted in offering more questions than answers. None of them dampened an undercurrent of optimism. "I find I can't live without hope," she said. "Good things happen that we can't believe."

One of Madeleine's dogs on top of the Star Watching Rock, Crosswicks, 1982.

Memories of Madeleine

by Barbara Stetson

Barbara Stetson teaches sailing in New York Harbor. She is a contributor to SAIL Magazine *and* The New Book of Sail Trim. *She took Madeleine's CHS workshop for several years, beginning in 1994.*

My friend Katherine talked very excitedly about the writing class she took each fall with Madeleine L'Engle. She mentioned it so many times that I decided to find out what she was talking about. I had not yet read any of Madeleine's books. Her most famous book, *A Wrinkle in Time,* came out when I was no longer a child. After reading *A Wrinkle in Time,* I signed up for Madeleine's class right away. I did not realize at that time how much it was going to change my life.

For me, what I learned from Madeleine was finding my own voice. How Madeleine helped her students find their voice is a mystery to me. She created an atmosphere in the classroom in which her students felt safe to find that deeper part of themselves. She would often choose Biblical topics for a writing assignment, like rewriting a psalm in our own words. Then she would tell us not to spend more than one half hour writing. The effect was that we wrote spontaneously. And some of her assignments led to ideas that years later became full novels!

Because she knew how to go to a deeper place, she had a way of inspiring others to do so, too. Her comments were always fascinating. She would often tell us mystical stories, sharing her true life experiences, like a time when there was a phone outage in New York City, yet when she called the convent, the phone rang and someone answered; or how her dog did not like to walk down a certain street in Manhattan because it knew something bad had happened there. She was not afraid to go to that deeper place. She believed that spirituality was at the basis of all great novels.

One of her gems of wisdom was to listen to the characters and let them speak to you. After saying that, she might describe two very different characters and the assignment would be to write about their meeting. She also talked about letting a story cook. She said she had several stories cooking inside her head that were not quite ready to be written down yet. She possessed the golden thread of storytelling. She knew how to find that thread and let it tell the story. And that is what she was trying to teach us: how to find our own golden threads.

One of her assignments was to write a story that took place in a convent. I wrote a story in which Madeleine was the heroine. I didn't plan it. I was just having fun, and it came out that way. She was Sister Alyssa, the eldest nun at the convent. She was not sure that the description of eldest nun fit her, so I said in class I meant *wisest* nun in the convent.

I began the story with "It was a dark and stormy night at the Convent of the Saintly Anointed." This was a reference to the first line in Madeleine's book, *A Wrinkle in Time*. It was to let people know that the story was about her. In the story, Sister Veronica Marie wakes up during the storm. She hears a crash from somewhere downstairs. When she goes to investigate, she finds Susan, the newest novice, in the chapel praying. Accidentally, the gun Sister Veronica Marie is carrying goes off. This wakes up the other nuns, including Mother Mary Margaret. Just as Mother Mary Margaret is about to take charge of the situation, Sister Alyssa, an elderly nun, steps out of the elevator. She takes Susan under her wing and leads her back onto the elevator, saying that she was once young and scared, too.

The class gasped as I read the line that was taken from *A Wrinkle in Time*. Once the story got going the class was amused. After class, as Madeleine was passing by me, she said quietly, "Thank you." She was flattered at her portrayal as the wise nun who took the novice (us) under her wing. I smiled to myself and felt very special.

Madeleine *was* very wise, both in her books and in the classroom. She told us not to underestimate the reader. She said that she did not write children's books, but books with children as characters. She was reading about modern physics and quantum mechanics before she wrote *A Wrinkle in Time*. She believed in instant travel through space. It was the adults who first turned down her books. It was the children who understood what she was saying.

Madeleine understood the connection between modern science and God. She told us about the butterfly effect: that when something happens in one place in the universe, it affects something somewhere else in the universe. Her young fans picked up on the spiritual nature of her books and loved them. They had no problem with Mrs Who traveling through time and space. (Madeleine preferred the British spelling of Mrs Who without the period, but her American editor put the periods back in throughout the book, and it was too expensive to change once the book was ready for the printer.)

One of the gifts of being in her class was hearing Madeleine talk about her life. She was born down South. Her father was ill from World War I and had trouble breathing. Her mother was a very talented pianist. She was too shy to play on stage. They were older when Madeleine, their only child, was born. The focus in the family was on her father's illness. They moved to New York City, where Madeleine, who often had to entertain herself, discovered that she liked to write. She kept journals all of her life. She was a lonely child and lived in a world of imagination. She described herself as an awkward child who was not a good athlete. Her writing was so good that one of her teachers did not believe that she had written one of her assignments. She remembered her parents' parties, their guests and her mother playing the piano. They also lived briefly in Switzerland to help her father's lungs. This became the setting for her novel *And Both Were Young*.

Madeleine graduated from Smith College. While a student there, she was asked to write an outline for a novel as an assignment. She said that after doing the outline she never wrote the novel. She felt that in doing the outline, she had already revealed all the ideas, and there was no need to write the novel!

After college, she moved to New York City, where she acted in small parts in plays. She wrote her first novel, *The Small Rain*, backstage during that time. She also met her future husband, the handsome actor Hugh Franklin. She said the most devastating time in her life was when they broke up. He was not ready to get married. Fortunately, a year later, he came back into her life. They got married while the play they were in was on the road.

She told us how she and Hugh came to adopt their daughter Maria. A couple with whom they were friendly died. The mother had expressed a wish that if anything happened to them, Madeleine and Hugh would raise their daughter. Because it was not in writing, Madeleine was devastated that the child who was in so much pain was delayed for legal reasons for six months from coming to her. Madeleine always put other people's needs first. She raised her adopted daughter as her own. Her family became the inspiration for her Austin family series.

Madeleine hated to see other people suffer. She felt her own and other people's pain deeply. She did not believe that God wanted people to suffer. Yet she recognized that her best work came as a result of her struggles in life. Writing helped her deal with the pain in her life. And her stories became a gift to us.

She told us, too, how her husband had read every manuscript and helped edit her work. And she told us how she answered every letter that children sent to her, sometimes with the help of her granddaughters.

Madeleine affected my life on many levels. I loved discovering her books. She was a spiritual teacher. She was an amazing person to be around. She made her students feel part of a community, with our annual gatherings at her apartment and the writers' groups that formed out of her classes. One person from my writing group, Sister Claire Joy, joined the convent! During Lent, Madeleine and Dean Morton from the Cathedral of St. John the Divine would host evening discussions of different spiritual topics, and those brought us together again, too.

I am grateful that I learned to find my own voice in her classroom, for I feel that it is a gift that keeps on giving. I had always been a quiet, observant person before Madeleine's class. Now I am better able to share my ideas and thoughts with other people, both in conversation and in writing. I now have the confidence to feel that I have something worthwhile to say and that other people might be interested in hearing me. And I am glad to have had the chance to share these memories with you.

I have one final story about Madeleine. She talked about going into a trance-like state to write. Before sitting down to write, she would play the piano. Then her husband knew that she was writing when the music stopped. Madeleine may no longer be with us, but her music lives on in her books and in our memories of her.

Madeleine and Hugh, China, Spring 1986.

Separation from Stars

by Linda Champanier

Linda Champanier studied writing with Madeleine for several years, beginning in 1997. Author of fantasy short fiction, poetry, and essays, she co-authored three literary study guides published by Learning Links.

Separation from stars, which she described as the literal translation of disaster, was the topic the first time I heard Madeleine L'Engle speak in about 1985, in a Greenwich, Connecticut church. I had read her books for years, and loved her long before I knew her. Her strong voice, both in person and in her books, spoke of a God I recognized. I'm impatient with theology that tries to put God in a box, rigidly defined, thoroughly explicated, and clearly much more correct than other God boxes. But Madeleine's God didn't fit into anything less than all of time and space—with extra dimensions thrown in for good measure.

She never spoke of a God who was merely nice and loving—a God of kittens, sunshine, and rainbows. Madeleine's God set galaxies spinning, wound the clock of time, and created worlds born in earthquakes, thunder, and volcanoes. She recognized the paradox of a God who showed infinite love and very personal tenderness, yet seemed at times to be as remote and cold as deep space. Madeleine clearly said that she found much more of God in science than theology. There was nothing tentative in her faith. She was fearless and fierce in confronting the heartbreaking questions of how a loving God could allow the evil in the world to continue. Where was God when death stole children from their mothers' arms? Why did some people live with excruciating pain? I had been touched to read her story of walking on the street when a man came up and began hitting her with bags of cans. She described her struggle to find Jesus manifested in this person. Her words "pray when prayer seems dry as dust" gave substance to faith in the face of hopelessness and loss.

It was probably a decade later when I learned of Madeleine's participation in a panel during Lent at the Cathedral of St. John the Divine. We sat on folding chairs in a simple room, while Madeleine sat at a table with two or three other speakers and talked of the sacrifice of incarnation. She said there was far more to Christ's gift than His death. She pondered the profound surrender of a God who had been unbound by space, infinitely powerful and all knowing, making the choice to be born and live on earth. How could we begin to imagine the loss of God, becoming bound in a baby's body, completely helpless and thoroughly human? Listening to her was such joy. Afterward, my husband, Paul, and I walked in the gardens, marveling at the loud peacocks and contemplating miracles.

Another opportunity to hear Madeleine came when we found out at the last minute that Madeleine was going to be speaking at a church in Torrington, Connecticut. We set off to hear her, but really didn't know where we were going. I have no sense of direction when I'm driving. Paul, with his uncanny ability to get in a car and go where he wants without even a map, drove to Torrington, which neither of us knew, pulled up to a church, and said perhaps this was the place. It was. I was torn between awe and irritation at his ability to effortlessly find places. But I think that telling this story to our friend Claudia Carlson was how I learned about Madeleine's writing classes. She had gone to the classes for several years, and when she heard how much I admired Madeleine, she told me how to get on the list to enroll.

I was so excited that I hardly dared to hope I had gotten into the class, especially since my beloved Aunt Anne, also a writer and married to an Episcopalian priest, knew Madeleine. After the wonderful news came that I'd been accepted, she would often ask about "Our dear Madeleine."

I worked in Purchase in Westchester County, and needed to leave work early in order to get to class on time. I don't think I even asked permission. There was simply no question that I was going, so every week I rushed out and let the adrenaline get me through the traffic to the Community of the Holy Spirit on West 113th Street, then drove around the block until I could find an impossibly small parking place.

Who knew there were Episcopalian convents? I certainly didn't, and I had no idea what to expect. But I remember the transition every week from the frantic driving to the absolute peace of the service that preceded dinner and Madeleine's class. I walked upstairs to the simple chapel and tried to follow along with the singsong chanting that was far removed from my experience of Presbyterian or Methodist hymns. After the service, we filed downstairs to a room fragrant with cooking and sat at tables, Madeleine sitting among the students. There may have been talking, but this time also seemed quiet. I do remember Madeleine being quite pleased when cheese grits were served for dinner.

After the meal, we wound our way back upstairs by way of a different and twisting staircase, although Madeleine rode in a forbidding elevator. I was always curious about the dogs I could hear barking from behind closed doors. The room

Linda Champanier and Madeleine.

where we met was snug. We shifted to fit around the dark polished wood table, where Madeleine sat at the head. I know I'm remembering from a perspective of deep admiration, but she seemed quite literally to have a radiant presence, reminding me of George MacDonald's archetypal grandmothers. I was profoundly aware of how blessed I was to have the opportunity to share time with Madeleine and tried to absorb all the wisdom she had to share.

When Madeleine spoke about writing, it was apparent that she had found her passion. She wrote journals from the time she was quite young. As a lonely girl in boarding school, she found solace in writing. She could write her way through any problem in life, sometimes weeping as she wrote. I smiled as she gleefully described creating characters based on people who had angered her and then doing awful things to the characters.

She was serious about being published. The oft-told tale of *A Wrinkle in Time's* long journey to publication had a practical moral. Madeleine recommended avoiding disappointment by looking at sending out manuscripts as an attempt to collect rejection letters. One was only getting started at one hundred rejections. She also talked with absolute scorn about *A Wrinkle in Time* being a banned book, but I sensed that she was also somewhat pleased by the distinction.

I wish I had a much better memory or that I was organized enough not to have misplaced the notes I took, because I want to remember every word, but I still can hear her voice.

Madeleine said you can learn something from everyone. Keeping that in mind has come in very handy almost every day.

She was emphatic about truth. Writing didn't necessarily need to be fact, but it had to be true.

Her teachings often echoed her books, but hearing her speak the words brought them vividly to life. She had no use for the niceties of religious denomination, declaring, "God throws a big party." Once she was asked about the Biblical stance on homosexuality. She dismissed the question with a wave of her hand, saying there were two references that were among the long lists of rules in the Old Testament. But her eyes shone and her voice was powerful when she talked about God and the struggles of sustaining faith.

The format of the actual writing classes was simple. Madeleine would give an assignment every week, sometimes to use a list of words, once to compose a sermon. The following week, we returned with our writing and took turns around the table reading aloud. Madeleine had a wonderful gift for bringing out everyone's best. It was always safe to read, knowing that the critique would be respectful and kind. She was, however, absolutely insistent that we complete the assignments. She said that anyone could find 30 minutes a day for writing, and she pointed out that if one wrote just one page a day, in a year that would be a 365-page book. Madeleine also talked about the books she loved. She was pleased to share her November 29th birthday with C. S. Lewis.

Speaking of books, I noticed one day that someone brought a book to class for Madeleine to sign. Aha! I collect books quite fanatically. I had first editions of most of Madeleine's books, carefully wrapped in mylar covers. Madeleine agreed to sign them, so I started dragging a heavy bag of books to class each week and she patiently wrote a short note and signed each one. I was delighted when I found a British first edition of *A Wrinkle in Time* and ordered it from New Zealand. When it arrived, I happily brought it to Madeleine to sign. She opened the book, went straight to the first page, and emphatically crossed out part of the first sentence. I gasped, but she was adamant that the British editors had added "in a small village in the United States" to the end of the true first sentence, "It was a dark and stormy night." So, it may not exactly be the pristine copy for the usual collector, but now I have a Madeleine-edited first edition.

My connection to Madeleine was pivotal to one of my most important life choices. We struggle over the decisions we believe are significant, but often the greatest consequences cascade out of a casual choice. In May 1999, my daughter

Emily was going to graduate from Swarthmore College. As a celebration, Emily and I had planned to go to a weekend retreat workshop that Madeleine was going to give in Pennsylvania. The event was canceled at the last minute when Madeleine fell and broke her hip.

Instead of going to Pennsylvania, Em and I decided to spend the weekend in Woodstock, New York. We missed the exit for the New York State Thruway. As we drove along back roads, air rich with mown grass, I sighed about how much I missed living in the country. Em replied, "You can do anything you want." Somehow I believed it. I pressed against the window glass of a Woodstock real estate office, examining the houses for sale. A month later, I found my house, a little sagging, filled with clutter and with a maze of rooms that led into each other without hallways. I climbed the hill behind the house through goldenrod, sweet fern, and wild blueberry bushes. When I turned around, the house was out of sight and mountains stretched across the western sky. I grew a tap root and knew I was home. Amazingly, the stock my grandmother had left me fifteen years earlier had grown to the point where I could buy the house.

When Madeleine's class started again in September, I showed her pictures of Mombaccus Mountain, and told her about the wonderful blessing that her broken hip had precipitated. She loved my mountain and said it reminded her of her own Mohawk Mountain.

Paul and I once drove to Goshen to hear her speak at her own church. Although I'm sorry I never got to see Crosswicks, we were invited to visit Madeleine in her new house in Goshen one Saturday, when we had offered our car to help her daughter move. We had brunch in the large open room, encircled by windows open to the surrounding woods. She was interested to learn that Paul and I had met when we were in a play, and talked about meeting Hugh when they did theater together.

One of my favorite memories of Madeleine was her description of a conversation with her granddaughter, who one day asked her out of the blue, "Will everything be all right?" Another person might have tossed out a glib answer, but Madeleine gave the question the serious contemplation it deserved. She said she thought about the world and all its possibilities. Then she thought about the fourteenth century prayer by Julian of Norwich: "All shall be well, and all shall be well, and all manner of thing shall be well." She took a deep breath and summoned every ounce of faith, courage, and hope before she could say with honesty, "Yes, everything will be all right."

Now I have granddaughters of my own, and I think of Madeleine with her granddaughter when I talk with them. Isabella, nearly five, has been contemplating death lately. She told me how she cried when Great-Grandpa Mickey died, and she would cry when I died. But she took my breath away when she concluded emphatically, "And if my daddy was going to die, I would catch his life!" I think Madeleine would have loved hearing that. I'm very happy that my daughter Ellyn chose to name her daughter Clara Madeleine, so there is an echo for the future in my family in Madeleine's honor.

My final memory of Madeleine is a mystery and a joy. I've always loved to write, but my truest passion is painting. I can stay up all night painting without even feeling tired, and I love creating paintings that evoke stories from people who look at them. I'd shown Madeleine my paintings over the years and she always commented kindly. But one day she looked at me and said, "Do you think you're a better writer or a better painter?" I didn't even hesitate before saying "Oh, a better painter." And she tilted her head, raised an eyebrow, and said simply, "Do you?" I sometimes wish I had questioned her further, but mostly I'm content to cherish those two words.

The Secret of the Sea, by Linda Champanier, 30 x 36 inches, oil on linen, 2005.

Ousia

by Judith Haas

Judith Haas has edited and written devotionals, newsletters, magazine articles, and program curricula, and enjoys expressing herself through essays and short stories. Formerly a social worker for her county Board of Social Services in the Adult Protective Services unit, she serves on the board of several church and community service organizations. Judy took Madeleine's CHS workshop in the early 1990s.

Friendships can't all be lumped together! There are many different levels of friendships, but I've come to appreciate them all, each one in its own way. There are the acquaintance-friends: the man who sells you your morning cup of coffee (and puts in two sugars without asking), or the woman who washes your hair in the beauty salon. They call you by name, ask about your family, but they're not listed in your cell phone. Other friends are in your life just for a season. More rare, but very special, are the long-term "I've known you forever" kind of friendships. And then there are the people you know by their heart and soul, whether you are aware of the details of their lives or not. And that's how I knew Madeleine.

I first became acquainted with author Madeleine L'Engle through a small, local writers' group I joined. When Pam Leggett (a "blood-sister-friend-for-life" friend) asked me to become part of this group she was forming, it was hard to say no. I enjoyed writing as a hobby, but I was a novice. The idea of sitting in discussion with "real" writers was rather intimidating, but Pam assured me that the others in the group would be a lot like me—people who loved to write but were still a little insecure about their abilities as a writer. Pam modeled the group after the writers' workshop run by Madeleine that she had taken several times.

Our first meeting was almost comical. We were supposed to bring a piece we had written to read aloud to the others in our small group, but oh, how awkward we all were about doing that! No one wanted to be first. We used up half of our time together painfully avoiding the reading. Gradually, we began to open up and share our work, and it became very obvious that each one of us was gifted with a special voice that was unique and worthy. An interesting thing began to happen as we read aloud to each other: we started to share our personal lives as well. As we came to know each other better, it was easier to know how to encourage the writer in each of us, and we cheered each other on, in our writing and in our lives.

Right from the beginning I started hearing Madeleine L'Engle's name mentioned. We applied many of the same techniques that Madeleine used to encourage budding writers, and I soon learned that a few of our members had already taken Madeleine's workshops in New York. They talked of Madeleine in such a loving way, with a sense of awe, and they all looked forward to being able to enroll again sometime soon. I thought it would be nice to participate in such a workshop, but their unusual admiration had me curious about the woman herself.

I recalled having read Madeleine's book *The Summer of the Great-Grandmother* a few years earlier. Someone had given it to me to read when my older parents had first come to live with us due to their failing health. At the time, I thought it was a lovely book, but I did not yet grasp the fullness of Madeleine's message. Our little writers' group continued on through the months and seasons, and with the passage of time, my parents' health problems worsened. Life became more difficult for them, for me, and for our household. As I shared my travails with my group, there was a nudging in my head telling me to reread that book.

The Summer of the Great-Grandmother is an account of Madeleine's journey in discovering her mother and losing her mother at the same time. That is to say, in that long, last summer they shared together in Madeleine's home in Connecticut, and in the writing of that book, she came to know her mother from the heart in a way she had never known her before. She sees her as a child and comes to know her as a young wife, and she relates stories of her parents' lives together from Madeleine's own childhood years. In her journey she begins to see her mother, and her father, through the eyes of an adult, not simply from her own childhood memories. Most importantly, in the midst of her mother's increasing dementia and failing body, Madeleine discovers her mother's *ousia* (Greek)—that inner spirit that defined her mother.

I didn't have to reread the book after all. When I picked it up, Madeleine's message came flooding back to me. I scanned through the book, looking for the word *ousia*. That concept had been profound when I first read it, and yet it had slipped away to be rediscovered another day. In a great "aha" moment, I realized I was now traveling that same journey with my own parents.

Joining the nuns for dinner and evening Vespers before class was a new and spiritual experience for me. That service quieted my mind and opened my heart to God, and uniquely prepared me for the writers' workshop that followed.

Finally, in the upper room where Madeleine held the class, the small group of participants sat together around the huge, oblong conference table, and I was at last introduced to the woman I was already coming to admire on my own.

She was a Presence. When she was in a room, it was filled, but she did not dominate it and there was always room for friends. She sat at the head of the table, looking a little imposing to me with her short, close-cropped greying hair and austere expression. I was struck by her beauty, which radiated from inside out when she began to speak. She was, it seemed to me, a very free spirit—though I'm not sure she would describe herself that way. The whole experience felt very eccentric and intriguing to me, climbing up the stone stairways in the convent, our voices echoing, and settling into this upper room with eighteen strangers. Yet when Madeleine walked in the room and sat at the head of that table, it felt right and good.

I honestly don't remember the words she spoke that first night in her class, but I remember being captivated by them. When she gave us writing exercises to do at home, I looked forward to the challenge. Often I struggled to understand what she was trying to pull out of me in the assignments, but when it finally

Madeleine Greek line dancing at her granddaughter Charlotte's wedding, August 1996.

emerged, what a joyous feeling! As we listened to her critiques of our written assignments, we began to see things from her perspective. Week after week, she encouraged, poked and prodded, and challenged as we read our work aloud to the group. She said what she thought without hesitation, and her comments often made us dig down deep, explore, and try new ways of expressing our ideas. In the process, she shared some of her personal life with us, and we began to get to know some of her joys and struggles. But she was already visible from way down deep inside. We could already see her on the inside, if we looked.

Not long after the workshop was finished, my father died suddenly. Within two years, we discovered my mom was having her last summer with us in our home, and I thought of that book. And as Madeleine had done, I found myself listening to stories of my mother's childhood, many of which I had never heard before. She spoke of her hopes and dreams and of life in a different time. I could visualize her as an eight-year-old girl drinking from a garden hose, and then as a teenager, flirting coyly with boys—before she met my father. My father was one of those "bigger than life" people, and it seemed for so long that she had been "Alex's wife." It was hard for people to separate her from that role. But thanks to Madeleine, I recognized that I could do just that. I was discovering my mother's *ousia*.

During my parents' last years with my family, I watched both of them slowly lose more and more of their physical abilities. Life chipped away at them as they drew closer to their end on earth. But as they were physically fading, their true spirits glowed brighter, as if one could begin to see their souls. When all else fails, that is what is left: the heart and soul, that inner person whom God uniquely created. And I thought of Madeleine's book. I finally understood *ousia*.

But my discovery didn't stop there! Once I began to understand the sense of that core person, I could see it in others if I really looked. I began to look past what I saw on the outside, and to encounter the person God created on the inside. I had always been able to see that "God-created" person in my friend Pam, and some others, as well. Now I understood that really knowing someone is much more than knowing their favorite food or keeping their secrets. It means knowing their hearts. I was becoming more aware of my own *ousia* and was surprised to discover that it was beginning to make appearances in my written work. It was what Madeleine had been trying to pull out of me.

People knew Madeleine in many different ways. On the surface, most people would presume my friendship with her was the "for a season" variety. The world will remember her as a master writer and a gifted teacher. And she was a wife, a daughter, a mother, a friend, and probably many other things. All those things are important. But at the core of her—what remains when all that is put aside, and what matters most—is her soul, the woman God created her to be. That is the Madeleine I know best.

Madeleine, Child of God.

Madeleine, West Chicago, Illinois, early 1980s.

The Tallis Canon

Original text (verses 1–4) Thomas Ken, 1637–1711; added text (verses 5–6) Madeleine L'Engle; music, Thomas Tallis, c. 1505–1585. After singing the traditional words of the hymn, Madeleine enjoyed adding her own verses, such as the ones you see here.

All praise to God whose love gave birth
to galaxies and stars and earth.
All praise to light, to joy, to peace
to God whose love will never cease.

Teach me to live that I may dread
the grave as little as my bed
teach me to die that so I may
rise glorious on that awe-ful day.

Books by Madeleine L'Engle

1. *18 Washington Square South: A Comedy in One Act*, 1944
2. *The Small Rain*, 1945
3. *Ilsa*, 1946
4. *And Both Were Young*, 1949
5. *Camilla Dickinson*, 1951
6. *A Winter's Love*, 1957
7. *Meet the Austins*, 1960
8. *A Wrinkle in Time*, 1962
9. *The Moon By Night*, 1963
10. *The Twenty-Four Days Before Christmas*, 1964
11. *The Arm of the Starfish*, 1965
12. *Camilla*, 1965
13. *The Love Letters*, 1966
14. *A Journey With Jonah* (a play), 1967
15. *The Young Unicorns*, 1968
16. *Dance in the Desert*, 1969
17. *Lines Scribbled on an Envelope and Other Poems*, 1969
18. *The Other Side of the Sun*, 1971
19. *A Circle of Quiet*, 1972
20. *A Wind in the Door*, 1973
21. *Everyday Prayers*, 1974
22. *Prayers for Sunday*, 1974
23. *The Risk of Birth*, 1974
24. *The Summer of the Great Grandmother*, 1974
25. *Dragons in the Waters*, 1976
26. *The Irrational Season*, 1977
27. *A Swiftly Tilting Planet*, 1978
28. *The Weather of the Heart*, 1978
29. *Ladder of Angels*, 1979
30. *The Anti-Muffins*, 1980
31. *A Ring of Endless Light*, 1980
32. *Walking on Water: Reflections on Faith and Art*, 1980
33. *A Severed Wasp*, 1982
34. *The Sphinx at Dawn*, 1982
35. *And It Was Good: Reflections on Beginnings*, 1983
36. *A House Like a Lotus*, 1984
37. *Trailing Clouds of Glory: Spiritual Values in Children's Literature*, 1985 (with Avery Brooke)
38. *Many Waters*, 1986
39. *A Stone for a Pillow: Journeys with Jacob*, 1986
40. *A Cry Like a Bell*, 1987
41. *Two-Part Invention*, 1988
42. *An Acceptable Time*, 1989
43. *Sold Into Egypt: Joseph's Journey into Human Being*, 1989
44. *The Glorious Impossible*, 1990
45. *Certain Women*, 1992
46. *The Rock That Is Higher*, 1993
47. *Anytime Prayers*, 1994
48. *Troubling a Star*, 1994
49. *Glimpses of Grace*, 1996 (with Carole Chase)
50. *A Live Coal in the Sea*, 1996
51. *Penguins and Golden Calves: Icons and Idols*, 1996
52. *Wintersong*, 1996 (with Luci Shaw)
53. *Bright Evening Star*, 1997
54. *Friends for the Journey*, 1997 (with Luci Shaw)
55. *Mothers and Daughters*, 1997 (with Maria Rooney)
56. *Miracle on 10th Street*, 1998
57. *A Full House*, 1999
58. *Mothers and Sons*, 1999 (with Maria Rooney)
59. *Prayerbook for Spiritual Friends*, 1999 (with Luci Shaw)
60. *The Other Dog*, 2001
61. *Madeleine L'Engle Herself: Reflections on a Writing Life*, 2001 (with Carole Chase)
62. *The Ordering of Love: The New and Collected Poems of Madeleine L'Engle*, 2005
63. *The Joys of Love*, 2008

About the Authors

Diane Amison-Loring was a member of the Community of the Holy Spirit for thirty-one years. A longtime children's book librarian, she lives and works in Connecticut. She has authored reviews for *VOYA* (*Voice of Youth Advocates*) and has served on the American Library Association's Newbery Award committee. She lives with her husband, Father Bill Loring, and their three cats. Bill and Diane enjoy traveling whenever possible.

Terryl Wiley Anderson is a Minnesota native who moved to Chicago to begin a twelve-year career as a professional ballet dancer. After teaching ballet for another six years, she left the arts to enter the business world as a sales representative, then a regional sales manager. Discovering a desire to write, Terryl returned to the arts and theater by writing and directing plays and skits. She and her husband live in New Jersey, where they are raising two adopted daughters. Terryl has recently begun work on her first novel.

Patricia McMahon Barry, a poet and attorney, lives in the Bronx with her husband, Robert, and dog, Sarah. Pat is a lector and Eucharistic minister at Our Lady of the Assumption Church in the Bronx and is active in several charities. On Pat's wedding day in 1998, Madeleine helped give her away and was her "mentor of honor."

Barbara Braver is a writer and editor who edited a book co-authored by Madeleine and Luci Shaw, *Friends for the Journey.* Barbara met Madeleine when assigned by a magazine to do a profile of her in 1985. In the years that followed, they became close friends. When Barbara's work brought her to New York and away from home and husband, she shared Madeleine's New York apartment for part of each week for a dozen years.

Kay Buckley, a close friend of Madeleine's for fifteen years, came to know her through All Angels' Church in Manhattan. She took many of Madeleine's New York workshops and assisted her in teaching others. Kay has published her poetry in magazines. She has also written a memoir about the remarkable life, and untimely passing, of her son, Rob, who died in 1993 at the age of twenty-seven. Kay taught science and health on a high school and college level for nearly three decades. She lives in Glen Ridge, New Jersey.

Claudia Carlson was born in Bloomington, Indiana and raised in many college towns across the U. S. She attended Stony Brook University, where she double-majored in English and Art History. She works as an award-winning graphic designer and illustrator (http://www.claudiagraphics.com) and lives in New York City with her husband, Jim Racheff, a playwright, and a dachshund and a calico cat. She has two grown daughters. Her first book of poetry, *The Elephant House*, was published by Marsh Hawk Press in 2007.

Dana Catharine lived in Mexico for many years and now lives in Brooklyn, New York, where she teaches Latin and runs the Summer Abroad program for her school. She is the author of *To Fly with the Swallows*, a book about old California, and co-author with Richard Larios of *La Causa*, a children's biography of Cesar Chavez. She contributes frequently to *Appleseeds*, a children's history magazine. She is presently at work on a memoir of her life in Mexico. She has two grown sons and three Mexican cats.

Linda Champanier studied writing with Madeleine for several years, beginning in 1997. The author of fantasy short fiction, poetry, and essays, she co-authored three literary study guides published by Learning Links. Linda won the Westminster College Chi Omega Fiction Award and was a member of the Riverwriters online writing group. In addition to writing, Linda is a painter and photographer whose work has been featured on several book covers. Her work as a commissioned portrait artist has been described as sensitive and evocative. She studied English and art at Westminster College in Pennsylvania and went on to study painting with Connecticut portrait artist Freda Dreany and, later, with Andrew Lattimore at Westchester Center for the Arts. Linda is a member of the Board of Directors of the Connecticut Society of Portrait Artists.

Carole F. Chase, a retired Presbyterian minister, was a professor of religious studies at Elon University in North Carolina from 1976–2001. During that time, she developed a course called "Religious Dimensions of the Writings of Madeleine L'Engle." A friend of Madeleine for two decades, she wrote *Suncatcher: A Study of Madeleine L'Engle and Her Writing* and compiled two books of Madeleine's works, *Glimpses of Grace* and *Madeleine L'Engle Herself.*

Stephanie Cowell won a few short story competitions in her late teens, then trained for a career as a high soprano. She sang in over thirty operas, formed a singing ensemble and a chamber opera company, and produced concerts and Elizabethan festivals. The translation of a Mozart opera sent her back to writing. She is the author of *Nicholas Cooke: Actor, Soldier, Physician, Priest; The Physician of London* (American Book Award, 1996); *The Players: A Novel of the Young Shakespeare;* and *Marrying Mozart,* which has been translated into seven languages and optioned for a movie. *Claude and Camille,* a love story about Claude Monet and his model/muse Camille, will be published in the spring of 2010. Stephanie is married to poet and Reiki practitioner Russell Clay. She has two grown sons and lives in New York City. Her website is http://www.StephanieCowell.com.

Jane Mylum Gardner, an elementary school art teacher in Wilson, North Carolina, is the author of two children's books, *Henry Moore: From Bones and Stones to Sketches and Sculptures* and *A Gift to America.* The friendships she formed as a result of meeting Madeleine have supported her and her writing through many life-changing events. "Because of Madeleine," she writes, "I am more open to acknowledging the multi-faceted parts of my own spirit, and to allowing space for invisible possibilities, and Guidance. Madeleine is still pointing the way."

Catherine Grace, CHS is one of the three leaders of the Community of the Holy Spirit. Sister Catherine Grace helped to create the Community's eco-spiritual education center and working farm at St. Cuthbert's House in the Melrose Convent, Brewster, New York. Through her numerous creative talents, her leadership, and her ministries for retreat work, spiritual direction, and education for sustainable living, she has touched many lives.

Judith Haas has edited and written devotionals, newsletters, magazine articles, and program curricula, and enjoys expressing herself through essays and short stories. Formerly a social worker for her county Board of Social Services in the Adult Protective Services unit, she serves on the board of a new non-profit social service organization, doing program development and organizational planning, and is active on church boards as well. She is married, with two grown children and three young grandchildren, and resides at the Jersey Shore.

Peggy Harrington, a poet, writer and close friend of Madeleine's, served as Arts Coordinator and Dean James Parks Morton's "right hand" in directing all events at the Cathedral of St. John the Divine in New York in the 1990s. In this capacity, Peggy welcomed to the Cathedral Nelson Mandela, Archbishop Desmond Tutu, famed aerialist Philippe Petit, musician Paul Winter, the Archbishop of Canterbury, and His Holiness the Dalai Lama, among others. In 1996, Peggy worked with Dean Morton to found the Interfaith Council of New York. She was a tireless worker for environmental sustainability and social justice, and also a gifted cultural critic of theater, art, and politics. A central figure in Madeleine's circle, she often orchestrated Madeleine's New York City functions and attended virtually all of them. Peggy died of pancreatic cancer in November 2005, leaving a beloved daughter, Susan, and many devoted friends, a number of whom are represented in this collection.

Sandy Hudson first became aware of Madeleine L'Engle in 1969, when she was required to read *A Wrinkle in Time* for a children's literature class. As she describes in her essay, seven words from *A Circle of Quiet*— "I was looking in the wrong mirrors"—changed her life. Sandy attended Madeleine's writers' workshops and retreats in monasteries, convents, colleges, and retreat centers in New York, Connecticut, Illinois, and North Carolina for over fifteen years. She lives in Westfield, Indiana, with her 24-year-old daughter, whose middle name, Saranam, came from *A House Like a Lotus*. Sandy operates a small chauffeuring business, and frequently reflects on the fact that almost everything she does now is a direct result of meeting, loving, and having been loved as a godchild by Madeleine L'Engle.

Dr. T. K. Hunter is a historian (M.A. & Ph.D., Columbia), art historian (M.A., Hunter College Graduate Art History Division), writer, consultant, and public historian. Her history expertise centers on the English-speaking Black Atlantic in the seventeenth and eighteenth centuries involving the movement of Blacks back and forth between Britain and the New World colonies. Her work frequently focuses on eighteenth-century English law and its effects in the matter of the liberty of diasporic Africans. She has been active in the discipline in a variety of public history capacities, acting as a consultant for the "Revolution" episode in WGBH-TV's production *Africans in America*, and as a speaker for Black History Month on African Americans in the Revolutionary period. In addition to receiving a variety of fellowships, Dr. Hunter has presented numerous conference papers and written a number of essays and book reviews. After teaching at Marymount, Columbia University, NYU, Western Connecticut State University, and Princeton University, she returned to teaching at Columbia at the Institute for Research in African-American Studies (IRAAS). Among her many projects, T.K. Hunter is currently working on a historical novel tentatively titled *Publishing Freedom* about the free African-American community in New York City in the early 1800s.

Claire Joy, CHS, is a member of the Community of the Holy Spirit in New York City. Before her call to the religious life she was an artist for thirty years, working in photography, television and AV production, 3-D animation, and graphic design. She now enjoys creating cartoons and writing a blog called "Flavor of the Month" at http://clairejoy.blogspot.com. Continuing her interest in sacred digital art, she has also exhibited on the Episcopal Church and Visual Arts (ECVA) website and contributed a visual essay on her "Eden Series." Sister Claire Joy is a firm believer that laughter is one of God's greatest gifts.

Katherine Kirkpatrick (editor) writes primarily for young adults, though she occasionally publishes reflective essays. She is the author of *Keeping the Good Light, Trouble's Daughter, Redcoats and Petticoats, The Voyage of the Continental, Escape Across the Wide Sea, The Snow Baby: The Arctic Childhood of Robert E. Peary's Daring Daughter* (A James Madison Honor Book, 2008) and a forthcoming archaeology book about Kennewick Man. An associate lay member of the Community of the Holy Spirit and a former New Yorker, she now lives in Seattle with her husband and two daughters. Her website is http://www.KatherineKirkpatrick.com.

Pamela Leggett was a close friend of Madeleine's and attended her workshops and retreats for many years. She began her career in creative therapies, which later led her into the world of writing. Now she lives in Montclair, New Jersey with her husband and daughter. They also own homes in Lima, Peru and New York's Adirondack Mountains. Both are used for service and retreats. Currently Pam and her family are hosting a mission project in Pisco, Peru, the site of the massive 2007 earthquake.

Judith Lindbergh's first novel, *The Thrall's Tale*, about three women in the first Viking Age settlements in Greenland, was a Book Sense Pick and a Borders Books Original Voices selection. Her work has appeared in *Archaeology* Magazine and in connection with the Smithsonian's exhibition "Vikings: The North Atlantic Saga." Also an accomplished photographer, Ms. Lindbergh's images of Greenland and Iceland have enjoyed several exhibitions, including one at the Cathedral Church of St. John the Divine in New York. She currently teaches creative writing in Maplewood, NJ and lives nearby with her husband and two sons. Her website is http://www.JudithLindbergh.com, and she blogs about writing at http://judithlindbergh.wordpress.com.

Shellen Lubin is a writer, director, performer, and master teacher of theater and music. She has written, directed, and appeared in numerous plays, musicals, and cabaret acts in productions, workshops, and readings all over New York City, where she lives. As a vocal and acting coach, she has taught and coached professionals for stage, screen, and recordings and has taught at a number of professional and private schools, including Marymount Manhattan College, Mannes College of Music, and Bennington College, her alma mater. Shellen also has an M.I.L.S. degree from Syracuse University, and writes a weekly think piece online called the *Monday Morning Quote* (http://www.mondaymorningquote.com). Shellen wrote to Madeleine for the first time when she was in college, starting a lifelong correspondence that also included one silent retreat and some extraordinarily fulfilling writing workshops. Her website is http://www.shellenlubin.com.

Genellen McGrath earned a Master's Degree in Library Science in the late 1970s, the same time period in which she married David McLaughlin and moved into the Walt Whitman Birthplace in Huntington, Long Island. It was there she started her career in public library service, which has taken interesting turns and twists along the way, including being a perfume sample maker, civic association president, technical writer, and network administrator. Occasional forays into writing workshops have taken her on houseboats (with leader Hannah Merker) and in convents (with Madeleine). Currently Genellen is the director of the Gold Coast Public Library in Glen Head, New York, a library she helped to create four years ago. A co-editor of the library's newsletter, she puts the lion's share of her creative energy into writing staff memos, board reports, and policies. Genellen, who still aspires to write, is also the parent of a son, David, and a daughter, Helen, through whose writing and blogging careers she lives vicariously.

Cornelia Duryée Moore feels privileged to have been Madeleine's friend and godchild for almost thirty years. She is a wife, mother, writer, director, and filmmaker. Her award-winning feature film *The Dark Horse* is currently in film festivals. Her Seattle-based production company, Kairos Productions, is currently in early pre-production on her second feature film, *Camilla Dickinson*, based on Madeleine's book *Camilla* (http://www.kairos-productions.com). The third dream described in her essay came to her on the morning that she prayerfully signed the contract to produce the film, after singing "St. Patrick's Breastplate" as was proper for the occasion. She is married to actor Terry Edward Moore, and is the proud and grateful mother of Tallis and Theo Moore. The Moores are owned by four cats, Tesseract, Tegwen, Smee, and Krevlorneswath of the Death Wok Clan, as well as a large black horse, Cobus (aka Taliesin).

Janet O'Connell has combined creative writing with positions in teaching, inner city missionary work, and day care management. "Working with people through the venue of creative writing," she says, "contributed significantly to my career successes in all of these fields." She has also worked as a consultant and trainer in the financial sector. Greatly influenced by Madeleine's workshops and friendship, Janet continues to pursue writing, particularly poetry, as she leads a community writers' group in the Adirondack Mountains in upstate New York. As a retiree, she also has more time to pursue her love of theology, music, and being a grandmother.

Elsa Okon Rael is a well-known playwright, lyricist, and children's book writer. Eight of her plays have been produced numerous times for decades, including eleven off-Broadway showings, and their scripts are available through Samuel French, Inc. Recent productions include her trilogy of plays based on Sally Hemings and her family at the Women's Interart Center and her play *Secret of O-sono* at the 86th Street Playhouse, both in New York City. Her new musical, *Last Lady of Stuyvesant Town*, will have its first professional review audition in early 2009. Elsa is the author of four picture books: *Marushka's Egg*, *What Zeesie Saw on Delancey Street,* and the American Library Association Sydney Taylor award-winners *When Zaydeh Danced on Eldridge*

Street and *Rivka's First Thanksgiving.* Elsa regards the group she met through Madeleine as "her family," and they in turn called her "Bubba Elsa." Dozens of writers who have enjoyed her warm hospitality over the years consider her apartment, in the center of Manhattan's Theater District, to be a second home. At age 82, Elsa is at work on her first novel, about the French resistance movement in World War II.

Evelyn Rein is a native of Alabama who lives in New York City with her husband. She has published travel articles and is currently working on a book of short stories. She is also a printmaker, an art medium that allows her to tell stories in a more tactile, hands-on manner.

Daria Rydzaj lives in New Jersey with her husband, two children, a lizard, a turtle, and assorted fish. She started her career as a chemist with a biology degree. She is the author of one technical publication, a short story, and many editorial essays in local New Jersey newspapers. In the 1990s, she regularly attended Madeleine's writers' group meetings in New York.

Luci Shaw, a close friend of Madeleine's for more than thirty years, has published nearly thirty books, including ten poetry collections; *Breath for the Bones: Art, Imagination and Spirit: Reflections on Creativity and Faith;* and *The Crime of Living Cautiously: Hearing God's Call to Adventure.* With Madeleine she authored *Friends for the Journey*, a book of essays and poems; *WinterSong*, a book of Christmas readings; and *A Prayer Book for Spiritual Friends.* As Senior Editor and later President at Shaw Publishers, Luci also edited a number of Madeleine's poetry volumes and reflective spiritual works, including *Walking on Water: Reflections on Art and Faith.* She is a frequent retreat facilitator and is Writer-in-Residence at Regent College in Vancouver, British Columbia, Canada. Her books have been translated into Japanese, Korean, and Dutch. A mother of five and grandmother to nine, Luci lives in Bellingham, Washington. Her website is http//www.lucishaw.com.

Sanna Stanley is a writer-illustrator and a fine artist who works in many mediums, including etchings and watercolors. She is a popular workshop facilitator in art and creative writing in schools on the East Coast. Her picture books are *The Rains are Coming, Monkey Sunday,* and *Monkey For Sale* (An ASPCA Henry Bergh Honor Book for Fiction and a Notable Trade Book for Young People). She also illustrated *Amistad: The Story of a Slave Ship* by Patricia C. McKissack. Sanna grew up in Zaire, Africa as the daughter of missionaries. She lives in Madison, Connecticut with her husband and son. Her website is http//www.two-ems.com/Sanna.htm.

Barbara Stetson teaches sailing in New York Harbor and has led groups to many regions of the world. A contributor to *SAIL Magazine* and *The New Book of Sail Trim,* she lives in New York City.

Claire Whitcomb the former editor-at-large of *Victoria* magazine, is a brand writer at Eileen Fisher. She has written five decorating and history books, including *Real Life at the White House*, co-authored with her father, John Whitcomb. She lives in Madison, New Jersey, with her husband and two children.

Phyllis White is a third-generation native-born California who was married to Jerry for more than fifty years, and has three children and three granddaughters. She is a graduate of University of California, taught elementary school, and worked as a volunteer in inner-city schools and with developmentally disabled people. She has written poetry, interviews, and reflective articles for church publications for many years. Since her husband has been gone, she spends about half of each year in Illinois with her daughter and son-in-law and the other half at her home in Southern California. She was a friend of Madeleine's for nearly twenty years.

Sally Lowe Whitehead is the author of *The Truth Shall Set You Free: A Family's Passage from Fundamentalism to a New Understanding of Faith, Love, and Sexual Identity.* She and her husband, Mel, live just outside the coastal town of Savannah, Georgia, where they own and operate a small business. They spend as much time as possible with six grown sons, four daughters-in-law, and six grandchildren. Sally studies and practices an ancient path of European Gnostic spirituality known as Laconneau and is currently at work on a new book about her experiences with that tradition.

Beth Vendryes Williams, an artist and art educator, lives with her husband, family, and dogs in Oyster Bay, New York. Inspired by Madeleine's writings, she attended workshops at CHS in New York. Madeleine's example and dialogue supported Beth's efforts to balance marriage, children, and painting; she currently paints for a couple of hours in the early morning before teaching! Beth's work acts as a metaphor for finding the holy in ordinary moments, people, places, and objects. Her art is in many private collections throughout the country. Beth's websites are http://bethvendryeswilliams.wordpress.com and http://www.bethvendryeswilliams.com.

Others who have contributed their time and talents to this book:

Cindy Kane, the line editor, is an author and editor of children's books and curriculum materials. Her books include *The Genie in the Book* and *Discovering the Titanic*, both written under her married name, Cindy Trumbore. She has edited numerous award-winning books, including *A Year Down Yonder* by Richard Peck, winner of the 2001 Newbery Medal. A former member of the Rutgers University Council on Children's Literature, she arranged for Madeleine to be the keynote speaker for the Council's 1990 conference. Her website is http://www.cindykane.net.

Andrea Simon, consultant for design and a contributing editor, has worked as a writer, photographer, editor, and manager on diverse projects, and was the co-owner of an editorial/production company that specialized in health-related educational materials. For the past several years, she has devoted her efforts to writing fiction and literary nonfiction, including her memoir/history, *Bashert: A Granddaughter's Holocaust Quest.* Several of Andrea's stories and essays have also been published, and she has been the recipient of literary honors including first place in the Ernest Hemingway First Novel Contest and the Authors in the Park Short Story Writing Contest. Specializing in archival black-and-white printing, Andrea's photographs have been featured in numerous venues. A resident of Manhattan, she has been a member of one of the Madeleine-inspired writing groups since the early 1990s. Her website is http://www.andreasimon.net.

Special thanks to: Christa Heschke and Edward Necarsulmer of McIntosh & Otis, Inc.; Mary Elizabeth, CHS, and all the sisters of the Community of the Holy Spirit; Sher Smith Ross, Alfred Tietjen, and Charlotte Jones Voiklis for their help.

19534669R00119

Made in the USA
Lexington, KY
22 December 2012